John H. Tullock

Clownfishes and Sea Anemones

Everything about Purchase, Care, Nutrition, Maintenance and Setting Up an Aquarium

With 78 photographs Illustrations by Erin O'Toole

BARRON'S

All inquiries should be addressed to:
Barron's Educational Series, Inc.
250 Wireless Boulevard
Hauppauge, NY 11788
http://www.barronseduc.com

International Standard Book No. 0-7641-0511-6

Library of Congress Catalog Card No. 98-18141

Library of Congress Cataloging-in-Publication Data
Tullock, John H., 1951–
    Clownfish and sea anemones : everything about purchase, care, nutrition, breeding, and behavior / John H. Tullock : illustrations by Erin O'Toole.
        p.   cm.—(A complete pet owner's manual)
    Includes bibliographical references (p.   ) and index.
    ISBN 0-7641-0511-6
    1. Anemonefishes. 2. Sea anemones. I. Title.
II. Series.
SF458.A45T85   1998
639.3'772—dc21   98-18141
                                      CIP

Printed in Hong Kong

98765432

About the Author

John H. Tullock holds a Master of Science degree from the University of Tennessee in zoology and microbiology. He is a full-time freelance writer. He is the author of five books on aquarium care of marine species. John Tullock is the founder of the American Marinelife Dealers Association, an organization of aquarium industry businesses that promotes environmentally sustainable practices and education for conservation awareness.

Photo Credits

Aaron Norman: cover, 8, 9, 10, 11, 12, 13, 14, 15 top right, 15 bottom right, 44 top left, 48 top left, 61, back cover; Scott W. Michael: inside front cover, 48 top right, 50, 51 top left, 51 bottom left, 51 top right, 52, 53, 54, 55 bottom left, 55 top right, 55 bottom right, 56 bottom left, 57 top left, 57 top right, 58, inside back cover; Paul Humann: 5, 15 top left, 15 bottom left, 16, 21 bottom right, 44 center left, 44 bottom left, 44 top right, 45, 48 bottom left, 51 bottom right, 68, 69; John H. Tullock: 55 top left, 56 top left, 57 bottom right; J. R. Shute: 59.

Important Notes

Electrical equipment for aquarium care is described in this book. Please do not fail to read the note below, since otherwise serious accidents could occur.

Water damage from broken glass, overflowing, or tank leaks cannot always be avoided. Therefore you should not fail to take out insurance.

Please take special care that neither children nor adults ever eat any aquarium plants. It can cause substantial health injury. Fish medication should be kept away from children.

Safety Around the Aquarium

Water and electricity can lead to dangerous accidents. Therefore you should make absolutely sure when buying equipment that it is also really suitable for use in an aquarium.
• Every technical device must have the UL sticker on it. These letters give the assurance that the safety of the equipment has been carefully checked by experts and that "with ordinary use" (as the experts say) nothing dangerous can happen.
• Always unplug any electrical equipment before you do any cleaning around or in the aquarium.
• Never do your own repairs on the aquarium or the equipment if there is something wrong with it. As a matter of principle, all repairs should only be carried out by an expert.

Contents

Preface

Clownfishes have captured the attention of marine aquarium enthusiasts with a tenacity rivaled by few other groups of fishes. Brightly colored, amusing in their habits, and easily maintained even in small tanks, the clownfishes are among the best choices for the novice saltwater buff. Additionally, because they readily spawn in captivity the clownfishes are rapidly gaining in popularity among advanced hobbyists seeking a new challenge.

The association between clownfishes and certain large sea anemones has been recognized by biologists for many years. This symbiotic relationship, in which the fish seeks shelter in the stinging tentacles of the anemone and thereby gains protection from predators, is central to the life history and ecology of the approximately 30 species of clownfishes found in the Indo-Pacific region. Traits that contribute to the survival of the clownfish, and the maintenance of the clownfish-anemone symbiosis, are largely responsible for the ease with which these fish adapt to home aquariums. Since clownfishes in nature are rarely found more than a meter's distance away from the anemone host, they accept confinement more readily that wider-ranging species such as tangs and butterflyfishes. Because clownfishes feed on plankton snatched from the water column, they can be fed a wide variety of commonly available aquarium foods. And because they are naturally more tolerant than most other reef fish, they can survive the minor mistakes inevitably made by inexperienced aquarists.

Unlike the majority of fish species found in the coral reef environment, clownfishes lay eggs that are attached to a solid surface near the host anemone, rather than casting their offspring into the open sea. In the 1980s, clownfishes became the first marine aquarium fish to be propagated in commercial quantities. Today, several hatcheries supply a growing percentage of the clownfishes that are purchased by marine aquarium hobbyists in the United States, and more and more amateurs are reporting success in breeding and rearing clownfishes in their homes. This trend has added an exciting new aspect to the hobby of marine aquarium keeping.

I have been an avid marine aquarist for 25 years, and have established and maintained marine aquariums for teaching and research purposes as well as for pleasure. I have worked with hundreds of species, and literally thousands of individual coral reef fishes. Yet, were I to choose a favorite, it would have to be the Common Clownfish, *Amphiprion ocellaris*. Bright as enameled porcelain in orange, white, and black, wearing a droll expression, and bobbing up and down above the waving tentacles of its host anemone, no other fish expresses the allure of the coral reef so eloquently. With the publication of this book, I hope to share that fascination with anyone seeking relaxation, understanding, and fun keeping clownfishes in the home aquarium.

John H. Tullock
Knoxville, Tennessee
May 12, 1998

A family of clownfishes and its host anemone, photographed atop an Indo-Pacific patch reef.

Understanding Anemonefishes

Aquarists, divers, and marine biologists have held a fascination for anemonefishes for many years. Anemonefishes, or clownfishes, are members of the damselfish family that have evolved the unique habit of associating with large sea anemones. An inkling as to how this relationship could have developed can be gained by observing the behavior of juvenile *Dascyllus albisella* damselfishes, which sometimes associate with anemones but later, as adults, do not. In the closely related *D. trimaculatus,* both juveniles and adults have been observed in association with at least eight species of anemones. (Fautin and Allen, 1992, see Useful Literature and Addresses, page 65). Among the anemonefishes, adults are rarely found more than a meter's distance from the host anemone.

The Sex of Anemonefishes

This unique dependence upon a scarce resource, giant sea anemones, has resulted in an equally unique way of coping with the problems of reproducing the species while avoiding inbreeding. All anemonefishes start life as males. Soon after hatching, larval fishes spend a period of time drifting with the plankton, feeding upon other tiny organisms. At metamorphosis, the juvenile anemonefishes must now locate and successfully join an established family of their own species that is already in residence in a suitable host anemone. As if this were not a sufficient challenge for a fish less than one inch (2.5 cm) in length, the resident male fish will drive off new arrivals that do not meet his criteria for adoption. Assuming the newcomer is accepted, he may yet never have the opportunity to fulfill his biological destiny.

The resident pair will consist of a large female and a much smaller male. (The dominant male will nevertheless be larger than the juvenile males that constitute the remainder of the clan.) When the breeding female anemonefish dies, her former mate rapidly develops into a functional female, and one of the juvenile males now assumes the role of breeding male. This arrangement guarantees that an anemone, once occupied, will never lack a source of eggs for continued propagation of the species. The pair may live to be over ten years old, and will during that time produce thousands of offspring, only a tiny fraction of which will survive to maturity. Thus, a newly metamorphosed fish may succeed in locating a suitable anemone, be accepted by the resident pair, and remain there for life as an undeveloped male. This life history, about which more will be said in a later chapter, might seem totally unfulfilling to us. We humans value individuals, while Nature values species. The anemonefish lifestyle has not only achieved the goal of species survival, but has led to the evolution of some 28 species of anemonefishes that are distributed throughout the Indo-Pacific region.

Gene Flow

Recruitment of juveniles from the plankton into established anemonefish clans ensures that gene flow occurs among various pairs of fishes within a given geographic area. In some cases, perhaps due to restrictions on the movement of larvae by prevailing currents, or distance to a suitable habitat, a particular variety of anemonefishes will be restricted to a comparatively small geographic area. The black and white form of *Amphiprion ocellaris*, found only around Darwin, Australia, is one example. This sort of species splitting is commonplace among organisms that live on "islands" (in this case the anemone), rather than occupying a contiguous area.

Captivity

Because they normally spend their lives in the restricted area near the host anemone, anemonefishes are "pre-adapted" to captivity. They are undemanding in their requirements, needing only appropriate water conditions and a suitable diet to thrive, and even spawn, in aquariums as small as 30 gallons (114 L). The anemone need not be present. (Read the information beginning on page 42 regarding keeping the host anemones before attempting to keep a symbiotic pair together.)

Gender Determination

The peculiarities of clownfish gender determination makes the process of acquiring mated pairs for aquarium breeding purposes quite simple: any two juveniles placed together in an appropriate environment will develop into a pair within several months. Many of the species of anemonefishes are available as captive-propagated specimens, with the Common Clownfish *(Amphiprion ocellaris)*, Clark's Clownfish *(A. clarkii)*, Tomato Clownfish *(A. frenatus)*, and the Maroon Clownfish *(Premnas biaculeatus)* almost universally available. Wild-caught clowns of all but the rarest species are still to be found in the aquarium trade, but the majority of specimens do not ship well and are becoming less and less popular as captive-propagated stock reaches the market.

Advantages of Rearing Anemonefishes

Anemonefishes are thus nearly perfect for the beginning marine hobbyist. Their relatively small size means they can be accommodated in a small aquarium. They are long-lived, surviving perhaps to the age of 15 years or more with proper care. All species are colorful, and their charming swimming behavior attracts interest from fish watchers of all ages. If kept under conditions suitable for the anemone, the fish and its coelenterate host will exhibit the symbiotic association that has long fascinated marine biologists and lay people alike. Being members of the damselfish family, clownfishes are tolerant of less-than-perfect water conditions, and thus afford the beginner a chance to make an occasional mistake without disastrous consequences. Anemones, however, are not so forgiving. Perhaps best of all, many varieties of clownfishes are available from hatcheries, meaning they are accessible in many shops and are reasonably priced. So ideal are clownfishes as aquarium fishes that some marine aquarium hobbyists have chosen to specialize in this group alone. While this may not be the route that you ultimately choose to take, you will learn from this book the basics for successful husbandry of the most popular of marine aquarium fishes. There are few better introductions to the fascinating hobby of marine aquariums than clownfishes.

The Species of Clownfishes

What Is a "Species"?

By training, I am a taxonomist. Classically, the science of taxonomy involves the identification, description, naming, and hierarchical grouping of species. Modern taxonomy also encompasses elucidating the evolutionary relationships among species, together with an effort to describe the ecological role of the species in its habitat. Zoologists, whose focus is upon species of animals, regard a "species" as consisting of populations of actually or potentially interbreeding individuals that are reproductively isolated from other, similar groups. The important concept embodied within this definition is that individuals of particular species do not under natural conditions interbreed with individuals assigned to a different species. Often, reproductive isolation results from the disjunct geographic distribution of similar species. In other cases, the existence of a physiological or behavioral barrier to cross-breeding may exist. Most of the clownfish species probably arose through geographic isolation of parental stocks.

Hybrids

Among anemonefishes, species have evolved that remain distinct in the ocean, although experimentation with captive individuals reveals that hybridization is possible. On the other hand, in the case of at least one natural "species," *Amphiprion leucocranos*, recent evidence (Nostrapour, 1997) indicates that it is a hybrid between *A. chrysopterus* and *A. sandaracinos*.

Colors

Complicating matters further is the fact that in some species, geographic color variants are known. For the novice, this may make the prospect of identifying a few of the species of anemonefishes somewhat daunting, but the majority of specimens seen in the aquarium trade can be readily identified on the basis of obvious, external characteristics, in particular the color pattern. A significant proportion of the anemonefishes now sold in aquarium shops—perhaps as much as 10 percent of the total—are produced in hatcheries. Identification of these, the most widely available and popular species, poses few problems, even for the novice. Nonscientists should note, however, that in addition to coloration,

Amphiprion leucocranos.

8

Amphiprion sandaracinos.

Amphiprion chrysopterus.

Amphiprion percula.

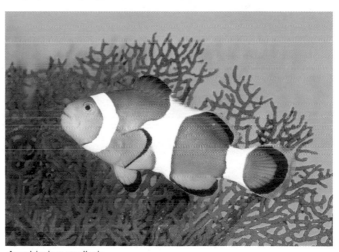
Amphiprion ocellaris.

details of body anatomy, such as the number of teeth or the number of dorsal fin spines, may be used by ichthyologists to separate species. This is why similar, even almost indistinguishable, species, for example A. ocellaris and A. percula, are nevertheless considered separate. The latter, which differs from its sister species in both dentition and fin ray counts, is restricted in its geographic range, while the former ranges over a much larger, though not overlapping, area of the Indo-Pacific. This is considered additional evidence that the two should be considered distinct, since interbreeding is unlikely.

Similarly, Clark's Clownfish, A. clarkii, has for years been incorrectly identified in the aquarium trade as

Table 1
Hatchery-Propagated Clownfish

Premnas
Maroon Clownfish, Gold-Striped Maroon Clownfish,
Spine-Checked Clownfish *(biaculeatus)*

Amphiprion	
Skunk Clownfish	*(allkalopisos)*
Clark's Clownfish	*(clarkii)*
Red Saddleback Clownfish	*(ephippium)*
Tomato Clownfish	*(frenatus)*
Cinnamon Clownfish	*(melanopus)*
Common Clownfish	*(ocellaris)*
Percula Clownfish	*(percula)*
False Skunk Clownfish	*(perideraion)*

Amphiprion clarkii, *Cebu, Philippines.*

Another, much darker color form of Amphiprion clarkii.

"Sebae Clownfish," because of the similarities in appearance between one of the many color forms of *A. clarkii* to the true *A. sebae*. The true *A. sebae* is much rarer in nature, and is seldom, if ever, seen in the aquarium trade. Another color variant of Clark's Clownfish is given the name "Black Saddleback Clownfish" by some aquarium dealers.

Tank-Raised Anemonefishes
Species of clownfishes listed in Table 1 are available from hatchery-propagated stock. Hobbyists may need to do some shopping to locate tank-raised clownfishes, but the effort is well worth it.

Wild Anemonefishes
Species listed in Table 2 are not currently available from hatchery stock, although limited numbers of some of these species may appear from time to time. Most specimens sold are therefore wild-caught, and precautions should be taken to ensure that you obtain a healthy, disease-free specimen.

General Comments on Clownfishes
Scarcely any other species of marine fish can compare with the Common Clownfish, *Amphiprion ocellaris*, as a perennial favorite. Everyone loves its bright colors, its amusing way of swimming, and its fascinating relationship with sea anemones. Common Clownfishes have been available as hatchery-propagated stock for several years now. Compared to wild-caught stock, captive-propagated fish adapt better to the aquarium and experience fewer problems with diseases and parasites. *Brooklynella*, for example (see page 33), almost always a problem for wild-caught clowns when they arrive on our shores, is seldom seen on tank-raised specimens.

Despite the fact that no anemone-fish is ever found without an anemone in nature, countless aquarium observations confirm that these fishes do not require an anemone in order to thrive, and even breed, in captivity. Planning an aquarium for clownfishes must give first priority to the needs of the anemone if you plan to keep the two together. Beginners are encouraged to not attempt to maintain the sea anemones, however, until they have gained considerable experience, as they are demanding.

Here are some specifics regarding the species listed in Table 1.

Premnas biaculeatus, *white-striped color form.*

Maroon Clownfish, Spine-Cheeked Clownfish
Latin name: *Premnas biaculeatus*

Keep only one maroon clownfish per tank, as this species is aggressive toward conspecific tankmates. Pair formation in captivity requires work. Hatcheries can supply pairs; a good route for the beginner to take if displaying a pair is the goal. The natural host anemone is *Entacmaea quadricolor*. Maroon clownfishes produce huge hatches, according to Bill Addison of C-Quest. He has a few pairs that lay egg clutches that are more than 6 inches in diameter (15 cm), and says that he has had more than 4,200 survivors from just a single spawn. A color form with bright yellow stripes is also available from hatchery production. This species seems prone to *Brooklynella* infestation, a problem that can be avoided by purchasing hatchery specimens.

Skunk Clownfish
Latin name: *Amphiprion akallopisos*

A nonaggressive species; although mature pairs may tolerate rival tankmates, keeping other fish with this clown is not recommended. Although *Heteractis magnifica* and *Stichodactyla mertensi* are the preferred

anemones, they are too delicate to be successfully maintained by any but the most experienced aquarists. The Skunk Clown will accept other anemones, including *Entacmaea quadricolor*.

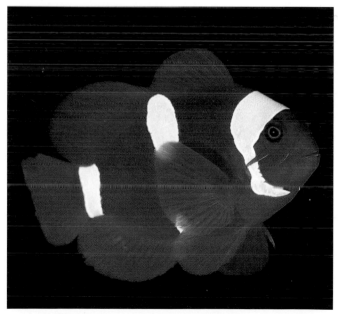

Premnas biaculeatus, *gold-striped color form.*

Table 2
Clownfish Generally Wild Caught

Amphiprion

Barrier Reef Clownfish	*(akindynos)*
Allard's Clownfish	*(allardi)*
Red Sea Clownfish	*(bicinctus)*
Chagos Islands Clownfish	*(chagosensis)*
Mauritian Clownfish	*(chrysogaster)*
Orange-Finned Clownfish	*(chrysopterus)*
Seychelles Islands Clownfish	*(fuscocaudatus)*
Moustache Clownfish	*(latezonatus)*
White-Bonnet Clownfish	*(leucokranos)*
McCulloch's Clownfish	*(mccullochi)*
Black-Footed Clownfish, Maldives Clownfish	*(nigripes)*
Oman Clownfish	*(omanensis)*
Brown Saddleback Clownfish	*(polymnus)*
Australian Clownfish	*(rubrocinctus)*
Orange Skunk Clownfish	*(sandaracinos)*
Sebae Clownfish	*(sebae)*
Thielle's Clownfish	*(thiellei)*
Three-Band Clownfish	*(tricinctus)*

Amphiprion allardi.

Amphiprion bicinctus.

Amphiprion akindynos.

Amphiprion chrysogaster.

Amphiprion chrysopterus.

Amphiprion polymnus.

Amphiprion latezonatus.

Amphiprion sandaracinos.

Amphiprion leucocranos.

Amphiprion thiellei.

Amphiprion nigripes.

Amphiprion tricinctus.

13

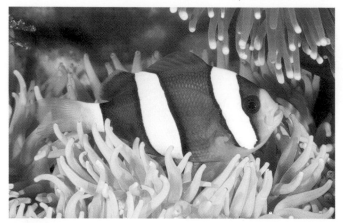

Amphiprion clarkii.

Amphiprion akallopisos.

Amphiprion ephippium.

Clark's Clownfish
Latin name: *Amphiprion clarkii*

Among the hardiest of all clownfishes, Clark's clownfish is readily available. Several can be displayed together until they reach sexual maturity, about 3 inches in size (7.6 cm). At this point, a pair will form and become aggressive. Spawns often yield more than 1,000 juveniles. It accepts any of the host sea anemones. This species is mistakenly sold as *A. sebae*.

Red Saddleback Clownfish
Latin name: *Amphiprion ephippium*

The only species that has no white stripe as an adult. Juveniles have three white stripes. The preferred host is *Entacmaea quadricolor*.

Tomato Clownfish
Latin name: *Amphiprion frenatus*

Keep only one or two together. Mature pairs may attack tankmates, a common trait among all species of clownfishes. It is a good choice for the beginner interested in spawning clownfishes, as it often spawns without encouragement from the aquarist. It accepts *Entacmaea quadricolor* and *Macrodactyla doreensis* as a host. Juveniles have three white stripes. By about four months of age, they have only one white stripe behind the eye.

Cinnamon Clownfish
Latin name: *Amphiprion melanopus*

Like other species, they can be displayed in groups until they mature. They prefer *Entacmaea quadricolor* as a host anemone. Two strains of cinnamon clowns, one with white stripes and one with stripes tinted in pale blue, are available to hobbyists as captive-propagated stock. Cinnamon clownfish pairs are usually available from the hatchery.

Amphiprion frenatus.

Amphiprion melanopus.

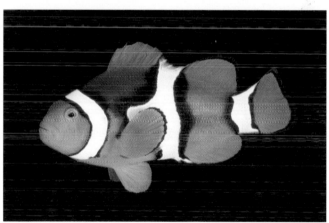

Amphiprion ocellaris.

Amphiprion percula.

Common Clownfish
Latin name: *Amphiprion ocellaris*

This is the most popular species. It is hosted by *Heteractis magnifica*, *Stichodactyla gigantea,* and *S. mertensi*. It will accept *Entacmaea quadricolor*, which is the preferred choice for the aquarium. It is readily available from hatchery production. The Common Clownfish is discussed throughout this book.

Percula Clownfish
Latin name: *Amphiprion percula*

Similar in all respects to the Common Clownfish. At least one hatchery now selectively breeds this species, and has developed some unique strains, one of which will be offered commercially. This may be the first marine fish color variety developed specifically for the aquarium market.

Amphiprion perideraion.

False Skunk Clownfish
Latin name: *Amphiprion perideraion*

This is another nonaggressive species that is not to be trusted when breeding. Its natural hosts are *Heteractis crispa*, *H. magnifica*, *Macrodactyla doreensis*, and *Stichodactyla gigantea*. In the aquarium, *Macrodactyla* is the best choice.

Marine Aquarium Basics

A proper aquarium for clownfishes should fulfill several important functions:
- It should provide enough space for a pair of fishes or a small family group.
- Environmental conditions required for the fishes to grow and eventually reproduce should be created.
- If the fishes are to be accompanied by an appropriate anemone, the aquarium should cater primarily to the ecological requirements of the latter.

Size Considerations

Because our discussion is limited to a single, well-known family of fishes, it is relatively easy to give precise recommendations concerning what size aquarium to consider. This will also depend upon the number and, to a lesser extent, the species, of clownfishes that you select.

Note. Only one species can successfully be maintained as adults in an individual aquarium. While individual clownfishes of different species may occasionally share an aquarium in peace, this is more likely to happen when the tank is very large, anemones for both fish species are present, and the fishes cannot see each other.

In all cases, a larger aquarium is more easily maintained than a small one. Thus, a 120-gallon (454 L) or larger system would be ideal for any family group (five individuals) of any species of clownfishes, together with appropriate tankmates. Cost considerations may influence tank selection, of course, since larger tanks are more expensive to set up and maintain than smaller ones.

Table 3 shows recommended aquarium dimensions for several possible system designs.

Since the aquarium will weigh about 10 pounds (4.5 kg) per gallon when filled, it will need a sturdy support near both electricity and a sink. The tank should be made entirely of glass or acrylic. You will also need a cover, which is usually supplied with the tank.

Filtration, Lighting, and Temperature

In addition to the tank itself, you will also need a filtration system, a lighting system, and a temperature control system. You should give considerable

Table 3
Recommended Aquariums for Clownfish

Fish Population	L	W	H	Gallons	A_s/V
Pair, minimum	36	12	18	30	14.4
Pair, ideal	36	18	22	58	11.2
Family, minimum	48	18	22	75	11.5
Family, ideal	48	24	24	120	9.6

thought to the selection of these components, as appropriate water conditions are essential to the survival of tropical marine fishes and invertebrates. There is a tendency to regard the clownfish as "tougher" somehow than its anemone. The fish will indeed tolerate suboptimal conditions more readily than its host but this does not imply that continuous exposure to such conditions is desirable. Clownfishes in their natural habitat are seldom found more than a meter away from the anemone host. Water conditions, temperature, and lighting cycles will thus be the same for both. Perhaps the only way in which anemones are exceptional, compared to the resident fishes, is their requirement for high light intensity (see page 22). While they do not require high-intensity lighting, fishes nevertheless are displayed to their best advantage under bright illumination.

Sunlight plays an important role in the nutrient recycling process that naturally occurs on coral reefs, and this fact has important implications in the selection of aquarium lighting. If any of the aquarium inhabitants are of the sort that carry out photosynthesis—and this includes the clownfish host anemones—lighting must be of high intensity and of a suitable spectrum. If these organisms will not be included in your aquarium, the simple fluorescent lighting fixtures that are sold in aquarium stores are quite satisfactory.

Nutrients

When you think about filtration equipment for any marine aquarium,

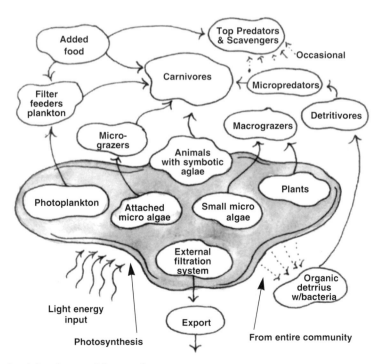

Food web in a large public aquarium.

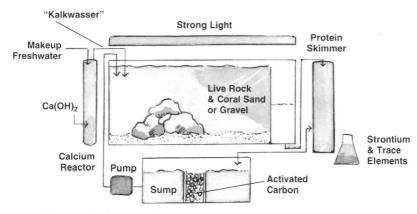

Diagram of a Berlin-style system.

think about nutrients. In the waters around coral reefs, there are not many nutrients. The novice saltwater enthusiast must never forget that all of the life forms inhabiting the marine aquarium come from the waters around coral reefs. Most of your work when you care for your marine aquarium will be involved with removing nutrients.

Nutrients are, of course, essential for the survival of living organisms; however, one of the special features of the coral reef environment is the paucity of nutrients in the water. Reef organisms have developed extremely efficient ways to capture, and in many cases to recycle, most of the available nutrients, with the result that the bulk of the nitrogen, phosphorus, and organic carbon present in the reef habitat is found in the biomass, not dissolved in the water. In the aquarium, a closed system and an ecologically incomplete environment under the best of circumstances, excess nutrients accumulate from the moment living organisms are added. This accumulation results in a decline in the water quality of the system. If nothing is done to reverse this process, water conditions will soon deteriorate to a point outside the range of tolerance of

the life forms, and they, in turn, will fare poorly. Filtration is therefore necessary to prevent, or at least retard, this gradual worsening of the water conditions. Filtration, combined with water changes and the judicious application of certain tank additives, enables the aquarist to maintain aquarium water in good condition almost indefinitely.

Filtration System

All any filtration system can do, really, is to extend the useful life of the water in the tank. And no filtration system, no matter how sophisticated, can eliminate the need for partial water changes. All filtration methods are applied with the intent of preventing changes in the chemistry of the aquarium water that would render it unsuitable or stress-producing, for the inhabitants of the tank. After 20 years of experience with marine aquariums, I have concluded that a "natural" system offers the beginner the greatest likelihood of success.

"Natural" filtration systems rely primarily on the good judgment of the aquarist, a protein skimmer, and ample quantities of live rock. Developing good judgment about marine

19

aquarium husbandry requires some hands-on experience, but this disadvantage is outweighed by the fact that the "natural" method is an ideal approach to a small, low-budget marine system.

Biological Filtration

Ammonia, nitrite, and nitrate are components of the biological filtration process. Proteins, found in every kind of food that might be eaten by a fish or an invertebrate, contain amino acids. Once metabolized, these eventually reach one of two places: the proteins of the animal that consumed the food, or the water, as excreted ammonia. Fortunately, nitrifying bacteria can be cultivated in the aquarium, and these will convert the toxic ammonia first into nitrite and then into nitrate. These beneficial bacteria are introduced into the aquarium along with live rock, which we will discuss shortly. Tests for ammonia and nitrite are used to determine if the important, bacteria-mediated processes, known collectively as "biological filtration," are proceeding correctly. Tests for each of these compounds should always be zero.

Nitrate

Nitrate, the primary end product of biological filtration, may be tolerated, with the degree of tolerance varying with the nature of the organism. You should test your tank for nitrate on a weekly basis, and carry out water changes with sufficient frequency and in sufficient amounts to keep the nitrate concentration rather low, around 20 ppm or less, if possible. Nitrate itself is not toxic; however, the accumulation (or perhaps depletion) of other compounds as the result of too infrequent a schedule of water changes may lead to harmful effects on the aquarium's inhabitants that are often incorrectly attributed to nitrate. The measurement of nitrate accumulation, therefore, can be used as an indicator of the need to perform a partial water change. It does little harm, in my view, to think of nitrate accumulation as dangerous, even though this is not strictly correct. The point is that the condition of aquarium

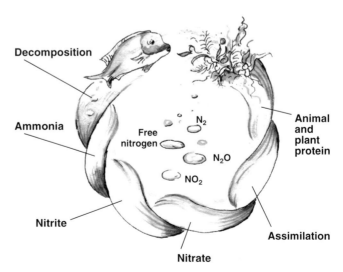

Schematic representation of the nitrogen cycle.

water changes over time and these changes are generally undesirable. Potential problems can be prevented by partial water changes.

Skimming

Protein skimming, also known as "foam fractionation," works together with the beneficial bacteria found on live rock to help maintain a low concentration of dissolved organic matter. All skimmers work on the same principle. Tank water is mixed with fine air bubbles, creating foam within the skimmer. Organic matter dissolved in the water tends to collect on the surfaces of the bubbles. As the foam builds up, it rises to the top of the skimmer, and spills over into a collection cup, eventually filling the cup with a greenish-brown, slightly viscous liquid that can be periodically discarded.

When choosing a skimmer, bear in mind that you will pay for two features:

1. A skimmer that can be hidden away, rather than taking up room in the tank itself, will cost more, since such an external skimmer must be leakproof.

2. A skimmer that uses a venturi valve to create the air/water mix will cost more than one that uses an air pump and air diffusers to achieve the same result. Venturi-type skimmers offer the advantage of relatively little maintenance, compared to air-operated types, which need new air diffusers every three or four weeks.

My experience with skimmers has been that the recommendations made by skimmer manufacturers, regarding the size tank for which the skimmer is appropriate, are generally reliable. There are hundreds of skimmers from which to choose; when in doubt, buy the larger model. It is not possible to "over-skim" the aquarium, and even a small, inefficient skimmer is probably better than none at all. Just make sure that you carefully follow the manufactur-

A protein skimmer (Courtesy Aquarium Systems, Inc.).

er's instructions regarding how to install and operate the skimmer properly.

The skimmer should be adjusted so that a relatively small amount of rather "dry" foam collects in the cup. It may take a few days, and adjustments may have to be made, to achieve the

Anemones thrive in the nutrient-poor waters around coral reefs.

21

Table 4
Recommended Lighting for Clownfish/Anemone Aquariums

Tank Capacity (gallons)	Lumens	Lighting
30	~3,300	Two (min.) or four (ideal) 30-watt fluorescent lamps
58	~5,000	Four 30-watt fluorescent lamps, or one 175-watt metal halide lamp
75	~6,700	Four 40-watt fluorescent lamps, or two 175-watt metal halide lamps
120	~8,900	Two 175-watt metal halide lamps

desired result. The exact adjustment will vary from one tank to another. Most beginners adjust the air supply or flow rate too high, so that clear water, not dark, viscous foam, collects in the cup. Start with a setting that seems too low at first, and note how the foam builds up after a period of time has elapsed. It may take several

Metal halide lighting system (Courtesy Energy Savers Unlimited, Inc. and That Fish Place).

Table 5
Fluorescent Lamp Specifications

Wattage	Length (in.)
20	24
30	36
40	48

Multiple lamp fluorescent lighting system (Courtesy Energy Savers Unlimited, Inc. and That Fish Place).

days for foam to begin collecting in the cup. With only a little experience, you will get the hang of it. If the tank is new, very little foam may collect, because only a small amount of material is present for the skimmer to remove. This does not indicate that something is wrong with the skimmer, only that the water does not yet contain much organic matter.

Lighting

Even if your tank will be one with no special lighting needs, consider the selection of the lamp as well as the fixture. Fluorescent lamps—the replaceable white tubes that fit into the light fixture—can vary in two ways, by wattage and by type. A fluorescent fixture is designed to accommodate lamps of a certain wattage. Lamps of differing wattages are usually of different lengths (see Table 5), and only the correct wattage will fit the fixture. For a given wattage, however, there may be many types of lamps. Fluorescent lamp types are identified with a variety of brand names, and with a coded designation printed on one end of the lamp. Different types vary in their brightness (intensity) and in the spectral quality ("color") of the light they produce. These characteristics are not important for a simple aquarium with no photosynthetic organisms.

Lighting is a critical consideration if you plan to keep photosynthetic organisms, including sea anemones. For them, you should choose a fixture that permits you to place several fluorescent lamps over the tank, or alternatively select a metal halide lighting system.

Table 4 presents minimum light intensities in lumens for each of the four tank sizes discussed earlier in this chapter. Included in this table are suggested lighting systems that will provide an appropriate level of intensity.

Use a timer to control the lights, creating a consistent day-night cycle of 10–12 hours of light and 14–12 hours of darkness automatically; otherwise, flip the switch on the light fixture on a regular schedule. Some fluorescent light fixtures require modification in order for them to work with a timer. If you need to modify the fixture, consult an electrician; it's relatively easy and inexpensive to do.

Temperature Control

Temperature control is important to the success of the clownfish aquarium. Purchase a heater of sufficient wattage to keep the aquarium at a constant temperature of 75–80°F (24–27°C). About three watts per gallon is usually satisfactory. The higher the wattage for a given number of gallons being heated, the faster the temperature of the water will rise when the heater is on. Sudden temperature shifts are to be avoided; therefore, do not select a heater that is of a higher wattage than that recommended.

Chillers

You may require a chiller if the tank does not remain below 80°F (27°C), except for brief periods. A chiller can represent a significant investment, but, if necessary to keep the tank in the proper temperature range, it is an indispensable component.

An aquarium chiller (also called a "fluid chiller") operates in essentially

the same manner as your refrigerator or air conditioner. A refrigerant gas is compressed by an electrically driven compressor, which results in the gas losing energy—its temperature goes down. The compressed gas flows through a heat exchanger, where it picks up heat from the surrounding medium, in this case water from the aquarium that is being pumped through the exchanger. The gas carries this heat back toward the compressor, and on the way encounters an expansion valve, which allows the gas pressure to drop. As the pressure drops, the gas gives up heat to a radiator, which, in turn, dispels the heat into the surrounding air with the aid of a fan. This is a relatively simple process to describe, but actually building a refrigeration unit requires considerable precision in the machine shop.

A chiller does not "create cold." Rather, it removes heat from the aquarium water. The rate at which a particular chiller removes heat determines its efficiency. Heat is measured in BTU's (British Thermal Units). One BTU is the amount of heat required to raise the temperature of one pound of water by 1°F. Thus, the higher the BTU rating of the chiller, the faster it will lower the temperature of a tank of given size. A

An aquarium chiller (Courtesy West Coast Aquatics).

Chiller Selection Chart (Courtesy West Coast Aquatics.)

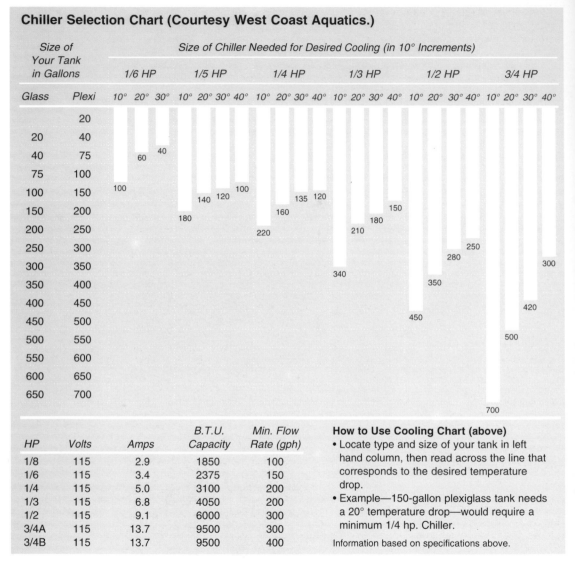

Size of Your Tank in Gallons		Size of Chiller Needed for Desired Cooling (in 10° Increments)					
Glass	Plexi	1/6 HP	1/5 HP	1/4 HP	1/3 HP	1/2 HP	3/4 HP

Chart values (gallons at which bars reach): 20, 40, 60, 40, 75, 100, 100, 140, 120, 100, 135, 120, 180, 160, 150, 220, 210, 180, 250, 280, 340, 350, 450, 300, 420, 500, 700

HP	Volts	Amps	B.T.U. Capacity	Min. Flow Rate (gph)
1/8	115	2.9	1850	100
1/6	115	3.4	2375	150
1/4	115	5.0	3100	200
1/3	115	6.8	4050	200
1/2	115	9.1	6000	300
3/4A	115	13.7	9500	300
3/4B	115	13.7	9500	400

How to Use Cooling Chart (above)
• Locate type and size of your tank in left hand column, then read across the line that corresponds to the desired temperature drop.
• Example—150-gallon plexiglass tank needs a 20° temperature drop—would require a minimum 1/4 hp. Chiller.

Information based on specifications above.

chiller with a high BTU rating will keep the tank at a constant temperature with less use of electricity and less wear and tear on the compressor than will a chiller of lower BTU rating. Unfortunately, a particular chiller's BTU rating often can only be determined in actual use of the chiller, which is seldom prac-tical if you are merely considering a purchase. Your dealer, or a chiller manufacturer, can help you with this. The calculated BTU rating for a chiller (1/5 horsepower) was 2800 BTU in a one-hour trial I carried out using a 120-gallon (454 L) aquarium system. The most efficient chiller designs will have a high BTU rating, do not feature a movable heat exchanger, and have sufficient capacity for the size tank on which they are installed.

Accessories

You will need an assortment of accessories for aquarium maintenance chores. Items such as buckets that will be in contact with aquarium water should be clearly labeled and used only for this purpose, in order to avoid inadvertently contaminating the aquarium. I suggest treating aquarium equipment as you would treat food-handling equipment in your kitchen. By the same token, if you would deem a particular container suitable for food storage, it should also be acceptable for storing aquarium water, dry salt mix, and so on. Suggested list of maintenance equipment

• Five-gallon (19 L) buckets, with lids, for storing and handling seawater. You will need at least two, and perhaps several, depending upon the size tank you have.

• A plastic container of 30 to 50 gallons (114–189 L), for mixing and storing seawater. (Plastic garbage cans work well; choose one with a snug-fitting lid.)

• About 6 feet (1.8 m) of clear vinyl hose, for use as a siphon. (Aquarium stores carry siphons fitted with a long tunnellike accessory that is very useful for removing debris.)

• Clear, rectangular plastic containers of various sizes for capturing and moving aquarium specimens. Aquarium stores often use "catch cups" made just for this purpose. Do not use nets for moving marine fishes and invertebrates, as you risk damaging them. Also, never remove specimens from the water; this can also damage them.

Two other types of equipment should be considered as part of your clownfish aquarium system. Neither is absolutely necessary, but each confers important benefits that you may not want to be without. These are wave makers and automated dispensing devices.

Wave Makers

A wave maker is an electronic timer that allows switching alternately between two small, submersible pumps (also called "powerheads") placed in the tank, simulating surge and turbulence found on a coral reef. This effect is important for sessile invertebrates such as anemones, which depend upon water movement to carry away wastes and to bring them oxygen and possibly food particles. Fishes often align themselves so that they are facing into the direction of the current flow. The value of this behavior is that food items are more likely to be swept toward them.

Automated Dispensing Devices

There are several designs for automatic dispensing devices. All of them accomplish the same thing: adding small amounts of water or tank additives on a regular, programmed basis. Such equipment is usually used to add water to make up for evaporation losses, or to add chemical supplements. You can, of course, do these chores manually, but automation helps, especially if you are not always conscientious.

An automatic dispensing pump (Courtesy Champion Lighting and Supply).

HOW-TO:
Treating a Parasite Infestation with Copper

Before administering any copper treatment to your clownfishes, remember these important points:
• Copper is toxic to most invertebrates. You must not treat with copper in a tank containing invertebrates.
• In higher concentration, copper is also toxic to fishes. If you do not properly monitor the copper level in the treatment tank, and maintain in within the limits prescribed, you run the risk of harming or killing the fishes with the copper itself.
• Success in treating a marine fish infested with either the *Cryptocaryon* (white spot, ich)

or *Amyloodinium* ("oodinium," marine velvet) parasites depends on many factors, including correct diagnosis and prompt, correct action on the part of the aquarist. The methods explained below have proven effective in practice by aquarists all over the world; nevertheless, the fish may not survive a bout of disease despite your best efforts.

Diagnosis
Many marine fishes probably die of easily treated parasite infestations because of failure on the part of the aquarist to notice anything wrong until it is too late. Observe your fishes carefully every time you are watching the tank, and learn how to tell if something is wrong.
Symptoms of the two most common parasitic infestations that affect marine fishes are

similar; therefore, it is customary to assume that both parasites are present, and to treat with a medication effective against the most deadly of the two, *Amyloodinium*. If you observe any of the symptoms listed below, take prompt action. *Amyloodinium*, especially, can kill fishes rapidly.
1. Rapid, shallow breathing;
2. Scratching, hiding, refusal to eat or other abnormal behavior;
3. Any evidence, such as gasping at the surface, that would suggest that the fish is having trouble breathing.
Since poor water quality can produce some of these symptoms, as well as exacerbate problems with parasites, always test the aquarium water carefully for improper conditions and correct if necessary before attempting treatment.

Treatment
The only effective way to treat the *Amyloodinium* parasite is to add a controlled amount of copper to the water. To do this, you will need a copper medication that contains ionic (not "chelated") copper. Such medications are a solution of copper sulfate in water. Adding one drop of a 10 percent solution of copper sulfate in distilled water per gallon of water in the treatment tank will approximate the correct dosage. An accurate copper test kit is nevertheless essential to determine the exact dosage.
Testing for copper requires care, because the effective concentration is low and the color change chemistry used by the available test kits is difficult for the eye to distinguish. Inaccu-

Successful treatment of a parasitic condition depends on a correct diagnosis.

rate testing will lead to failure in treatment.

I recommend a "hospital" tank of 20 gallons (76 L). This size is adequate for a pair of mature clownfishes. Filtration should consist of a hang-on-the-back power filter, fitted with a soft foam block for biological filtration. This filter can be conditioned by running it on your display aquarium for at least a month before moving it to the treatment tank. Install a heater and maintain the same temperature as in the display aquarium. Add two or three short sections of PVC pipe to provide shelter for the fishes; otherwise, the tank should be bare. Illumination from the room lighting is usually adequate for observing the fishes' progress

The treatment procedure is straightforward. Add enough copper solution to the treatment tank to give a test reading of 0.20 ppm. Maintaining this level of copper for two weeks beyond the disappearance of symptoms in the fish should effect a cure. Symptoms of labored breathing may disappear within hours after copper is administered; however, the fish will not recover completely for several days.

Most commercially available copper medications are formulated to approximate the correct concentration when a certain number of drops of medication are added to a certain number of gallons of water. These instructions assume that the tank is completely bare and free of calcium carbonate (lime)-containing materials. In a typical display tank, where shells, crushed coral, coral rock, and so on provide an abundant supply of lime, copper added to the tank will combine with the lime and be removed from the water. This results in lowering the reading on the copper test kit, another reason why it is best to treat the fish in a separate, bare tank. (PVC pipe sections make good hiding places for fishes being treated with copper.) Check the copper level in the treatment tank every two or three days, adding more solution if needed to maintain the correct concentration.

Additional Tips

When doing water changes on a tank treated with copper, make sure to correct the copper level after the water change.

If the fishes begin to dash madly back and forth or to struggle at the surface of the tank as if trying to escape, you have probably overdosed with copper. Do a large water change (50 percent) immediately—minutes are important.

Many kinds of chemical filtration, including activated carbon and protein skimming, may remove copper from the water. Use of chemical filtration of a hospital tank is obviously not desirable during copper treatment. Make certain, however, that you maintain proper biological filtration, aeration, and water movement in the treatment tank.

Copper impairs the fish's immune system so it is crucial that you give recovering fishes the best possible care in terms of water quality, diet, and freedom from crowding and harassment.

Water Conditions

Every marine aquarist must learn how to test aquarium water, and how to interpret the test results. These skills are essential for success in keeping fishes.

Marine aquarists who intend to keep clownfishes and sea anemones will need to be familiar with the following tests:
- ammonia
- nitrite
- nitrate
- pH
- alkalinity
- copper (maybe)
- calcium
- iodine

Regardless of which brands of test kits you buy, follow the instructions for their use *precisely*. Always rinse test vials thoroughly, ideally with distilled water, after each use, and rinse the vial with the water to be tested prior to each use. Do not store test reagents for more than a year.

In addition to chemical tests, purchase an accurate hydrometer and an accurate thermometer. The hydrometer and thermometer measure specific gravity and temperature, respectively. These two numbers are related, and are of great importance to marine organisms.

Specific Gravity

Measuring specific gravity allows one to estimate the salinity of the water, if the temperature is also known. "Salinity" refers to the amount of dissolved solids (salts) in the water, and, in a typical sample of ocean water is 3.5 percent or 35 parts per thousand (ppt). For water of a given salinity, the specific gravity reading varies with the temperature. At 75°F (24°C), the specific gravity of water at a salinity of 35 ppt is 1.0260.

Water

Strangely, aquarists do not give much thought to the quality of the fresh water that they use to prepare synthetic seawater, and most use plain tap water. I recommend strongly that you do not use tap water, as, unfortunately, municipal tap water and well waters are frequently unsatisfactory for aquarium use. This is due to the presence of pollutants that, while not deemed harmful for drinking purposes, can cause problems in the marine aquarium. Algae nutrients such as phosphate and silica, toxic metals such as copper, and a host of other compounds may all be found in "pure" tap water. I recommend that all water used for the marine tank be purified in some way.

For hobbyists with smaller aquariums, it may be best to purchase distilled water at the grocery store. If you need significant amounts of purified water, however, it is much cheaper in the long run to purify tap water via reverse osmosis (RO). This technique uses water pressure to force tap water through a special membrane, in effect "straining out" pollutants and producing, in most practical applications, water that is about 90 percent free of contaminants.

Test kits (Courtesy Aquarium Systems, Inc.).

RO units have two drawbacks. Water is produced drop by drop, with typical units producing about 25 gallons (95 L) of water per day, so a reservoir is needed. Also, about 4 gallons (15 L) of wastewater are produced for every gallon of product water; however, the wastewater can be used for cleaning or irrigation purposes.

If the tap water is very contaminated, some troublesome compounds, such as phosphate, for example, may remain in the product water in a large enough amount to cause problems in the aquarium. If this turns out to be the case in your community, RO water may need further purification by the use of *deionization*. This technique involves the use of special chemical resins to absorb undesired components from the water. The addition of a deionization filter to an RO system can result in purified water comparable to glass distilled water. Deionization can also be used as the sole means of water purification, dispensing with RO altogether, but this is a more expensive option, as the special resins must be periodically replaced, and they are costly. The advantages of using deionization alone are that water is produced on demand, not drop by drop, and there is no wastewater production.

pH

The degree of acidity or alkalinity of the aquarium water is measured as pH. Seawater is alkaline, and has a pH of 8.3. As acid is added to seawater, the pH drops, with the minimum acceptable reading being about 7.8 or so. Acid is a by-product of the biological filtration process referred to above. In addition, when carbon dioxide is released into the water as a result of respiration by fishes or invertebrates, it reacts with water to produce carbonic acid, thus, the tendency in any aquarium is toward a decline in pH.

A hydrometer (Courtesy Aquarium Systems, Inc.).

Maintaining the correct pH can be accomplished by regular water changes, or through the addition of buffering agents.

Alkalinity

Alkalinity (synonyms: "buffer capacity," "KH," "carbonate hardness") is a measure of the resistance of the water to a change in pH as acid is added. It is expressed in "milliequivalents per liter" (meq/l) and should be maintained at about 3.5 meq/l or above. If the alkalinity of the tank is at this level, it will be easier for the correct pH to be maintained. Proper pH is important to the respiration of fishes. Marine fishes depend, as do you and I, upon a specialized pigment, hemoglobin, in their blood to carry oxygen to their body tissues. However, there is no special carrier for carbon dioxide, a toxic by-product of respiration. Carbon dioxide, therefore, must escape from the fish's body directly into the water via the gills, and the rate at which it leaves

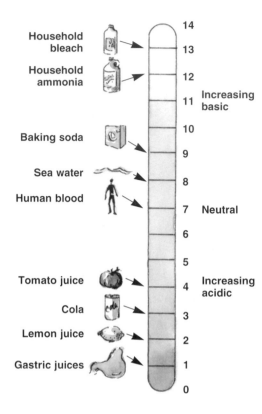

Household bleach — 13

Household ammonia — 12

11 Increasing basic

Baking soda — 10 / 9

Sea water — 8

Human blood —

7 Neutral

6

5

Tomato juice — 4 Increasing acidic

Cola — 3

Lemon juice — 2

Gastric juices — 1

0

14

The pH scale.

suffocates, despite the fact that there is abundant oxygen available.

Allowing the alkalinity of your aquarium to decline significantly may spell disaster for the tank's inhabitants. Carbon dioxide buildup can also occur due to insufficient gas exchange (usually resulting from poor water circulation) or overcrowding.

Phosphate

You may or may not need to test for phosphate. Only if you have a problem with undesirable, or excessive, algae growth is phosphate of interest. Phosphate concentrations above the limit of detection for most test kits (about 0.05 to 0.10 ppm) are often associated with algae "blooms." Each aquarist has an opinion as to the amount of algae growth that is considered desirable. Algae growth is not harmful. Indeed, many fishes, including clownfishes, appreciate green filamentous algae to nibble on. However, if you determine that you have too much algae, a phosphate test kit will be an important tool in dealing with it.

Marine algae exist in considerable variety. Some species of green, red, and brown algae, commonly called "seaweeds," are cultivated by aquarium hobbyists, and make suitable additions to the clownfish aquarium. Clownfishes may even nibble on these algae. Good choices are *Caulerpa*, with many species to choose from, and the calcified genus *Halimeda*. These algae flourish under conditions that are suitable for clownfish host anemones. Many other types of marine algae may sprout from live rock, or may appear in the aquarium unexpectedly. As a general rule, filamentous or slimy, mat-forming types that spread rapidly and overgrow desirable organisims constitute the problematic species. Keeping phosphate levels below 0.05 ppm seems to be the most effective way to control an algae "bloom," as such ram-

the fish is determined in part by the amount of carbon dioxide already present in the water surrounding the fish. In seawater of sufficiently high alkalinity, carbon dioxide is converted to the harmless bicarbonate ion, and all is well, but as the alkalinity falls, carbon dioxide can accumulate, making it increasingly difficult for the fish to eliminate this gas from its body. As a result, therefore, carbon dioxide begins to accumulate in the fish's blood. Unfortunately, the fish cannot cope with this situation indefinitely, and its blood pH eventually declines. When this happens, the hemoglobin loses its ability to carry oxygen, and the fish pant growth is often called. Sudden changes in the quality or amount of lighting, or a major disruption to the system (as might result from a prolonged power outage, for example), may be followed by an algae bloom. Sometimes, a particular alga will persist for several months, despite all attempts to eradicate it, and then disappear again for no apparent reason. I would caution beginners that taking drastic action, such as tearing down the tank and scrubbing the algae off the rocks in an effort to eradicate algae, generally fails to control the growth and may do more harm than good.

Copper

Sooner or later, you may have to deal with a case of saltwater "ich" (Cryptocaryon) or of "coral fish disease" (Amyloodinium). The most reliable, effective treatment for a fish infected with either of these microscopic parasites is to add copper to the water. To do this correctly, you will need a copper test kit and a spare "hospital" tank, as well as a solution of copper. Fortunately, clownfishes are seldom subject to these problems after they have settled into the aquarium. Most problems occur with newly acquired specimens.

Calcium

Seawater contains about 400 ppm of calcium; some seawater mixes provide only about half this amount. Adding a calcium supplement, in amounts determined by testing the water for calcium on a regular basis, is important for many types of marine animals. Thus, it is wise to keep the calcium concentration at natural seawater level.

Iodine

Found at a concentration of about 0.1 ppm in seawater, iodine is required by invertebrates. It is removed by protein skimming. For aquariums with a large invertebrate population, regular testing and addition of an iodine supplement will probably be required to maintain the natural concentration of this element.

Record Keeping

Buy good test kits, use them on a regular basis, and keep a written record of the results. Record the following information about your tank in a log book:
• date
• test(s) performed and results
• supplement(s) added and amount(s)
• temperature
• specific gravity
• amount of water changed
• species and size of fishes or other animals added
• incidents of death or disease, treatments, and results
• any comments or observations you think pertinent

Regular testing, good records, and consistent maintenance are the keys to a successful marine aquarium. While routine maintenance duties are an essential part of marine aquarium keeping, do not make the common mistake of constantly "fiddling" with the tank. Develop a maintenance program that places minimum demands on your busy schedule, and, above all, stick to it. Regular, appropriate maintenance will make the difference between having a marine tank that is a pleasure to own, and having continual problems. Following is a suggested aquarium maintenance plan.

Daily Maintenance

• Feed fish once or twice, choosing with care both the type and amount of food. (see HOW-TO: Feeding Clownfishes, page 34).
• Give each of your fishes a quick health check. Is each one behaving in the normal manner for its species? Clownfishes should feed eagerly, have

clear, bright colors, and exhibit alert behavior. Some experience in observing healthy fishes will help you to judge the condition of your tank's inhabitants. Of course, if something is amiss, take prompt action.
• Note the temperature of the tank, and check to see if fresh water should be added to compensate for evaporation.
• Adjust the heater and add fresh water as needed. Distilled water or reverse osmosis water is preferable to tap water for this purpose. Always replace evaporated water frequently enough that you do not have to add more than a quart or two per 10 gallons (38 L) of tank water. Some aquarists simply add a little fresh water every day after experience has taught them how much to add, on average. An automated top-off system is recommended.
• Quickly check out all the equipment to see that everything is working properly.

Weekly Maintenance
• Test and log results for all water conditions. If needed, correct pH and alkalinity. Consider changing water if the nitrate is beginning to get too high. Adjust iodine and calcium appropriately by the addition of supplements.

• Clean the front glass, inside and out.
• Siphon out any accumulated detritus, simultaneously remove about 10 percent of the water, and replace it with new synthetic seawater.
• Empty the collection cup of the protein skimmer, and replace its air diffuser, if not using a venturi skimmer.
• Check the operation of all other equipment.

Less Frequent Maintenance
• Change the lamps in the light fixture about every nine months, unless using metal halide lamps, which maintain their brightness for several thousand hours.
• Every so often, you will need to do a water change that is larger than usual to lower the nitrate concentration of the tank. Since nitrate constantly accumulates, the trend will be for nitrate to increase, despite regular small water changes. Each tank is different in the rate at which nitrate builds up. You can determine easily when to do a major water change, if you test regularly and keep records. Plan on about 20 percent each month, and a 50 percent change twice a year.

Seawater Preparation
Every marine aquarist should be prepared to carry out water changes whenever desirable, by having a container of seawater on hand. Always make certain that new seawater is similar to the tank water in terms of its temperature, specific gravity, and pH before you add it to an established aquarium. A clean, covered, plastic trash can is ideal for storing seawater. If stored covered in a cool, dark place, such as a garage, basement or closet, seawater keeps indefinitely.

A little more than two cups of seawater mix will make 5 gallons (19 L) of seawater. Always use distilled or purified water for making synthetic

a) Trophont—
   parasitic stage
b) Tomont—
   reproductive stage
c) Tomont with
   developing tomites
d) Tomite—infective
   stage

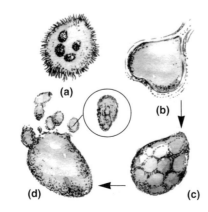

Cryptocaryon *life cycle*.

seawater. Buy dry salt mix in large quantities to save on its cost. It keeps indefinitely if stored in a tightly sealed container away from moisture, which promotes caking.

In practice, the maintenance of your marine tank will require about five minutes every day, an additional half hour or so every week, and about an hour every month. Every so often, perhaps twice a year, you'll need to spend an afternoon on a really thorough job of care.

Troubleshooting

Cryptocaryon and Amyloodinium

Clownfishes are remarkably free of problems when maintained under appropriate conditions. Stress, usually caused by improper care or a sudden change in water conditions, can result in any fish subjected to a less than optimal environment. The most common problem is caused by one or both of the protozoan parasites, *Cryptocaryon* and *Amyloodinium*. Symptoms include rapid, shallow breathing, and perhaps scratching, refusal to eat, and clamped fins. At the first sign of labored breathing, indicating that the fish's gills have become infected, the specimen must be transferred to a separate aquarium and treated with copper ions at a concentration of 0.2 ppm for a minimum of two weeks. Other treatments or failure to act promptly may result in the death of the fish.

Brooklynella

Although not often seen on tank-raised fish, *Brooklynella hostilis* is another protozoan parasite that infects wild clownfishes so commonly that it is often called "clownfish disease." Infected fishes produce copious skin secretions, making them appear as if they are peeling after a bad sunburn.

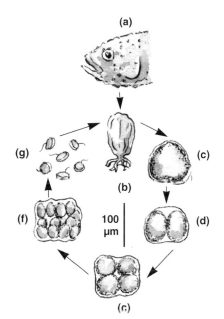

(a)

(g)

(b)

(c)

(f)

100 µm

(d)

(e)

a) Trophonts on infected fish
b) Trophont (enlarged)
c–f) Tomonts
g) Dinospore (resting stage)

Amyloodinium *life cycle.*

Left untreated, the infection is fatal. Fortunately, removing the infected fish to a separate hospital tank and treating it with a commercially available medication containing malachite green is usually effective in eliminating *Brooklynella*.

HLLE

Head and lateral line erosion (HLLE) is thought to result from improper diet. Limited available studies suggest that a deficiency of vitamin C and/or vitamin A may lie at the root of this condition. HLLE is manifested by a loss of pigmentation around the head and face, and becomes progressively worse. Prevention is easier than a cure, and involves simply feeding a balanced diet consisting of fresh or frozen foods.

33

HOW-TO:
Feeding Clownfishes

In the ocean, clownfishes feed on zooplankton, small animals, mainly crustaceans (copepods), which they pluck from the water column. This diet is supplemented with a proportion of algae. In captivity, this diet can be easily simulated, another reason for the widespread success aquarium hobbyists achieve with clownfishes.

Prepared Foods

Prepared foods, both in dry flake form and frozen, are available in any aquarium store. Several brands are intended for marine fishes such as clownfishes. Select foods with a high proportion of ingredients such as the kind of shrimp found at the grocery store, brine shrimp, mysid shrimp, krill, or amphipods. Individual organisms of any of these types are also offered in frozen form for feeding to marine fishes. Any of these can be fed to captive clownfishes, although I suggest you avoid the habit of feeding the same type of food over and over, which can lead to nutritional imbalances. Commercial foods should contain a relatively small proportion of plant-derived foods that may be variously listed as algae, kelp, seaweed, dulse, or *Sprirulina.* The relative proportions of the ingredients in a food can be estimated by simply reading the label. The components are listed by weight, in descending order.

Human Foods

Some common human foods can be used for feeding clownfishes. Any uncooked marine fishes, crustaceans or shellfishes can be chopped into pieces that will fit into a clownfish's mouth. Increasingly, marine algae, or "sea vegetables" are available, in both fresh and dried form, in markets, especially those that cater to a largely Asian clientele. These foods can also be chopped appropriately and fed to clownfishes.

What Not to Feed

With an abundance of excellent foods readily available to the clownfish enthusiast, there is little reason to resort to less-than-satisfactory substitutes. In particular, avoid feeding terrestrial foods, such as tubifex or black worms, beef heart, or vegetables such as spinach or broccoli. These are sometimes recommended in older books, but recent experience indicates that marine fishes do best if the diet is composed of ocean derived foods.

By maintaining a log of what you feed your clownfishes, you avoid the habit of feeding the same type of food over and over again.

Simple Aquariums for Clownfishes

Following are descriptions of two aquarium systems for clownfishes. The only major design difference between the two (apart from size) is the provision of bright illumination for a host anemone in the larger, more complex system. The living components of either system, with the exception of photosynthetic invertebrates, can for the most part be identical. The larger system can obviously accommodate a larger number of individual animals.

First, consider the identical set-up procedure for both tanks, bearing in mind that one is more than twice as large as the other and will thus require proportionately more substrate, live rock, seawater, and so on.

A Lagoon Habitat

The first theme I have chosen is a lagoon habitat, which will be housed in a 30-gallon (114 L) tank. I selected that tank size because it offers enough room to create an interesting ecosystem, but is small enough to be accommodated by a beginner's space and budget. In it will eventually be placed a pair of tank-raised Common Clownfishes.

Assembling the Equipment

You will need the following:
- a small protein skimmer
- a heater
- a fluorescent light strip with lamp
- a timer
- a cover for the tank
- a small powerhead

For testing water parameters, you will need:
- a thermometer
- a hydrometer
- test kits for ammonia, nitrite, nitrate, and pH

1. Rinse the tank thoroughly with fresh water, place it in its permanent position, and use a carpenter's level to make sure it is perfectly level. If the tank is not level, chances of a leak are increased.

2. Clean the glass carefully, then install a background. A solid color, black or dark blue, is the best choice. Use small pieces of tape to hold the background in place. To prevent

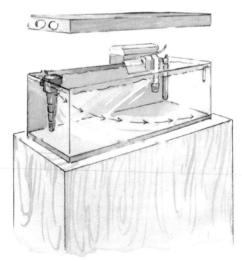

The clownfish aquarium with all equipment in place.

water from finding its way between the background and the glass, where it will evaporate and make a white stain, use duct tape to completely seal the background to the top frame of the tank; using one long piece of tape works best. Next, seal the other three edges to the tank in the same manner. Trim uneven edges. Replacing the background once the tank is set up is difficult, so it pays to do it correctly before filling the tank with water.

3. Install the skimmer, the power-head, and the heater, following the manufacturer's instructions, but do not plug in power cords.

4. Place the cover on the tank, install the light strip, and connect the light to the timer.

5. Once everything is in place, fill the tank with fresh water. Wipe up any spills, then connect all the equipment. Check to make sure everything is running properly.

6. Adjust the thermostat on the heater, following the manufacturer's instructions. You may have to check and readjust the thermostat several times over the next few hours until the correct water temperature is reached.

7. Leave the tank sitting overnight. The next morning, check to see that everything is still working well, and that

Adding salt mix.

no slow leak is evidenced by water accumulation. Leaks are not common, but do happen. Most manufacturers provide an appropriate guarantee. Check before you buy, and keep your receipt. If the tank does not leak within 24 hours, it probably never will.

Adding Salt

1. You need about 12 cups of dry salt mix for the 30-gallon (114 L) tank. You can simply add the salt to the tank and, wait a full 24 hours before you proceed. This is the only time you will ever add dry salt mix directly to the tank; doing so with animals present may kill them.

2. After 24 hours, check the specific gravity with your hydrometer. It should be between 1.0230 and 1.0240 at 78°F (26°C), or at 1.0260 75°F (24°C). If it is too low, add more salt mix, and wait at least three or four hours for it to dissolve before checking again. If the specific gravity is too high, take some water out and replace it with fresh water. It will take only a few minutes for the fresh water to mix in completely, and a new hydrometer reading can then be made. When the specific gravity is correct, you can mark the water level in an inconspicuous spot, using a permanent marker, to make it easy to tell when the water level changes as a result of evaporation.

3. Next, check pH. It should be in the range of 8.2–8.3 plus or minus 0.1 pH unit. Make certain the temperature, specific gravity, and pH are correct before you proceed.

Adding Live Rock

1. Order one pound of cured Indo-Pacific live rock per gallon of tank capacity. Starting with the larger, heavier, and/or less interesting pieces, build up a reef structure. Create an open arrangement that allows for water movement around each piece. Try to suggest a shallow patch reef by arranging the rock more or less in a semicircle. This will create a "stage" in the center of the tank in which the clownfishes are likely to spend a lot of time. Placing an isolated rock or piece of dead coral about the size of a softball in this area may be accepted by the fishes as a surrogate anemone. Clownfishes seem to remain in a restricted area instinctively. For the larger system, follow this pattern, also, leaving room in the center for a living host anemone.

2. Install powerhead(s), one for the small tank and two for the larger, hidden by the rock work, directing the outflow toward the front of the tank.

Adding Substrate

1. Wash the substrate material of your choice in a clean, 5-gallon (19 L) plastic bucket. Run tepid fresh water over the substrate, swirling it around with your hand. Pour off the water and repeat the process a time or two.

2. As each batch is rinsed, spread a uniform layer on the bottom of the tank. Don't worry if the tank becomes cloudy; it will clear up in a day or two.

3. When all of the substrate has been added, check to make sure that no small piles of sand have accumulated on top of the live rock. If so, just brush off the rock with your fingers. Now add, *without rinsing*, a pound (0.5 kg) of live sand per 10 gallons (38 L) of tank capacity. Spread this in a layer on top.

4. Appropriate substrate materials for a clownfish aquarium include aragonite sand, crushed coral rock, shell fragments, coral skeleton fragments, or a combination of these. The size of the grains can range from about 1/16 inch to 3/8 inch (1.6–9.5 mm) in diameter. See the discussions of individual species of anemones, beginning on page 43, however, as some have preferences as to the type and amount of substrate.

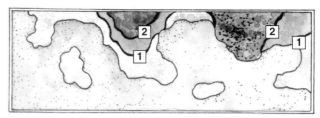

Top view of aquarium showing live rock placement.

1 = Contour lines showing elevations of rock structure between 5 and 10 inches.
2 = Contour lines showing elevations of rock structure between 11 and 16 inches.

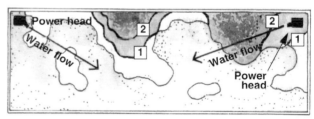

Front view of aquarium showing live rock placement.

Top view of aquarium showing powerhead placement.

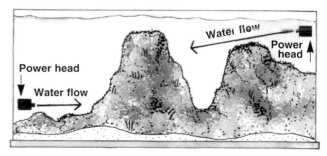

Front view of aquarium showing powerhead placement.

Rinsing substrate.

5. "Live sand" is harvested from the sea bottom. Particle size in live sand ranges from very fine up to about 1/16 inch (1.6 mm). Adding a small amount of this material to the aquarium substrate introduces tiny invertebrates and unicellular organisms. Many aquarists believe that including this component of the ecosystem provides numerous benefits, although I know of no scientific study that would directly support this contention.

6. Turn on the tank lighting, and adjust the timer.

7. Double-check to make sure the skimmer is working. (Little or no foam will be produced yet, but the skimmer column should be opaque with fine bubbles.) Recheck everything, and, if all seems well, leave the tank alone for a day or two, or until the water is completely clear. Now is a good time to begin your tank log.

Adding More Live Animals

Over the next few weeks, the tank will grow algae, so herbivorous species should be the first inhabitants. Wait until algae can be seen growing here and there. Add an assortment of species, chosen from the recommendations made in the chapter beginning on page 58, allowing about one animal per 2 gallons (7.6 L) of tank capacity. Wait a week before adding other specimens.

Completing the Ecosystem

1. After the tank has been home to snails and hermit crabs for a week or more, you can complete the system with additional invertebrates, chosen from among those described beginning on page 53.

2. Check the nitrate level each week and change water when it rises

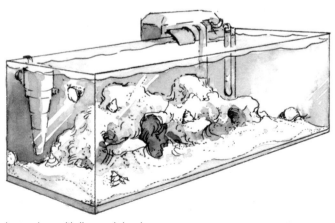

Completed aquarium with live rock in place.

above 20 ppm. This may be more or less often, depending upon individual circumstances. Check and record the pH every week. Check the temperature each time you observe the tank. Add distilled water to compensate for evaporation as soon as you notice that it has occurred. If you forget, and the water has evaporated far below the mark you made earlier, add distilled water a little at a time to correct the specific gravity by no more than 0.001 units per day. Use your hydrometer to determine how far the specific gravity has shifted in this situation, and to determine the rate at which your corrections are proceeding.

3. When the maintenance routine is firmly established, after the tank is about two months old, it is time to add the clownfishes. New specimens will require a few days to become accustomed to their surroundings. If the fishes hide and/or fail to eat for a short time, there is no cause for alarm. Healthy specimens should start feeding within three or four days. If there appear to be problems, consult with the dealer from whom you purchased the fishes.

4. Purchase a selection of foods at the same time you obtain the fishes. The dealer should tell you what the fishes were eating in his or her tanks, and should stock these foods for resale. Feed a small amount each day, observing carefully to make sure that all the food is consumed. If uneaten food remains on the bottom an hour after feeding, you have given too much. Remove the excess, and feed less the next time. Watch for normal behavior and check for appropriate tank conditions (correct temperature, equipment functioning properly) at each feeding.

Many people suggest that fishes can be introduced much earlier into the aquarium just described. I disagree and urge you to be patient, for the following reasons:

Clownfish at home in their miniature lagoon.

• It is an observable fact that tank conditions fluctuate during the early stages of establishing the system. This is probably due to the need to establish equilibria, or balance, among several biological processes that get underway as soon as living organisms are introduced.
• Even though captive-propagated, clownfishes are most susceptible to disease immediately after they are captured and transported from one aquarium to the other, owing to the inevitable stress this creates. Placing the already stressed fish into an unstable environment will only increase its stress, and in turn the likelihood of its developing a problem.

My best advice for satisfying the urge to buy some fishes is to set up a suitable quarantine aquarium, and place the fishes in it for observation and possible treatment while you are waiting for the main tank to become established.

It is worth bearing in mind that, properly cared for, your clownfishes can live for ten years or longer, so a few weeks' wait at this point hardly matters.

HOW-TO:
Selecting Cured Live Rock

"Live rock" is chunks of rock, often coral rubble, which is taken from the ocean with various species of encrusting organisms attached. Live rock reaches the aquarium retailer in much the same way that vegetables reach the grocer's shelves. Sometimes the product arrives freshly harvested and glistening with clean water when pulled from the shipping crate; perhaps an interesting arthropod or mollusk has tagged along, ambling about as if still basking under a warm sky. At other times, the journey has been arduous, and the product, smelly with an odor of putrefaction, is coated with slime. Mobile animal life either lies dead at the bottom of the box, or struggles feebly to avail itself of whatever moisture and oxygen might yet remain. As common sense would suggest, the longer the rock is out of water, the fewer survivors among its original complement of living organisms.

Types of Organisims Present on the Rock

Many organisms that were originally present on the rock are, surprisingly, able to survive the shipping process. Others, however, are not so hardy. This latter group of organisms, which includes various species of sponges, for example, cannot endure the rigors of travel, and they die. The die off of these organisms has noticeable effects when the rock is once again placed in water and decay of the organisms begins. Shiny, white growths of bacteria and fungi spread over the dead areas of the rock. Ammonia and organic matter are released into the water.

Curing

Curing live rock simply involves allowing the die-off and decay process to occur under controlled conditions, rather than having it occur in a display tank where the consequences for the other inhabitants would be decidedly negative. Freshly collected rock is first rinsed in seawater to dislodge sediment, and any obviously dead or dying organisms are removed. The rock is placed in holding tanks for a period of one week. At the end of that time, areas of decay will be apparent, and large decay spots can be siphoned off or removed with a brush. The rock is then transferred to a second group of holding tanks, after another rinsing in seawater, and is held there for an additional week. The end result is clean rock with desirable marine life still intact, but without dead or dying organisms that would pollute the display tank.

Using Only Cured Rock

Because of the potential for creating havoc with the display aquarium, aquarists must make sure that only cured rock is introduced. Rock that has only recently arrived from the collector has the most potential for problems; the longer it remains in the dealer's holding tanks, the less likelihood that additional die-off will occur when you take it home. "Healthy" cured rock has a clean, ocean smell, without odors of decay. The sniff test is a reliable way to assess its condition. Hobbyists should be forewarned that only a small percentage of dealers cure live rock before it is sold. The added effort involved in curing also adds to the rock's retail price, and you of course want to have some assurance that the product has been appropriately cured. The ideal way to accomplish this is to make advance arrangements and to visit the dealer several times during the curing process to inspect the rock yourself. Many hobbyists with whom I have corresponded have reported good experiences in purchasing cured live rock by mail order, motivated in most instances by the lack of a local dealer with curing facilities. The consensus among these correspondents is that the best suppliers offer a money-back return guarantee.

The correct (top) and incorrect way (bottom) to stack live rock.

Enhancements

I recommend a larger system, ideally of 75 gallons (284 L), for a small family group of clownfishes and, as the main attraction, a host anemone. The anemone requires bright illumination and I recommend installing a metal halide lighting system, instead of the single fluorescent lamp used in the previous example. Install a second powerhead, as mentioned earlier, and control both powerheads with a wave maker.

After this aquarium is established as described earlier, it will grow algae more abundantly, because of the brighter illumination. After about six or eight weeks, small patches of purple and mauve coralline algae should begin to appear here and there, and the brown, green, and red filamentous forms will be much less noticeable. Wait until this point to add the anemone or the tridacnid clams recommended in the chapter beginning on page 53. Otherwise, this system

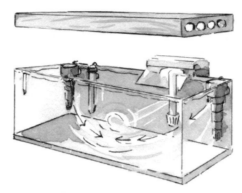

A larger tank requires two powerheads for additional circulation.

and the one in the first example, differ only in size.

The best choice in an anemone would be the Bulb Anemone, *Entacmaea quadricolor*. It could play host to a group of five captive-propagated Cinnamon Clownfishes, *Amphiprion melanopus*.

A clownfish pair with anemone are at home in the larger system.

Clownfish Host Anemones

Premature Loss

Few invertebrates are more widely available to aquarium enthusiasts than are sea anemones. Commonplace though they are, however, anemones are often poorly understood by beginners. Mistakes, such as failure to provide adequate light, allowing water conditions to deteriorate, or improper selection of tankmates, result in the premature loss of the majority of anemone specimens sold to hobbyists. This high failure rate is one reason that anemones should perhaps not be collected in such large numbers. An understanding of their requirements for successful aquarium care will enable you to decide if you should keep your clownfishes together with an anemone host. Since the ten clownfish host anemone species vary significantly in their adaptability to aquarium life, we will begin with a discussion of their classification, which requires us first to understand their anatomy.

Anemone Anatomy

Anemones are rather simple in structure, but there are some special terms used to describe parts of the anemone body that should be defined. Understanding the meaning of these terms will aid in identification of anemones that may be observed in aquaria. There are three regions of the anemone body:

Pedal disc. The *pedal disc*, or base, is flattened and either adheres tightly to a solid object, or is buried in sand. Providing soft sand, rather than a coarser substrate, may be important for anemones that bury themselves. The coarser materials may be irritating and prevent the anemone from locating itself properly. If the anemone cannot attach itself and expand its tentacles, it cannot receive sufficient light, oxygen, or planktonic food.

The column. Above the pedal disc rises the *column*, which may be hidden in the substrate in some species, and in others may be brightly colored and conspicuous. Some anemones possess little bumps, *verrucae*, on the column, and the presence or absence of these can be useful in identification. At the top of the column is the *oral disc*, with a central *mouth*, opening into the anemone's single body cavity, the *actinopharynx*. Sometimes the mouth is surrounded by ciliated grooves, the *siphonoglyph*, that aid in pumping water into the anemone. Recognizing this structure is helpful in identification.

Mesenteries. Between the inner wall of the actinopharynx and the outer body wall are the *mesenteries*, or *septa*, which are sheets of specialized tissue radiating outward from the wall of the actinopharynx (complete mesentery) and radiating inward from the body wall (incomplete mesentery). In the digestive cavity of the anemone, the complete mesenteries terminate in *mesenterial filaments* that aid in digestion and internal water movement. In some anemones, these end in tightly coiled filaments called *acontia*, which may be expelled in defense, although this is not the case for any of the clownfish host species.

Tentacles. Surrounding the mouth are the anemone's most notable features, the *tentacles*, of which the number, size, and arrangement are important for identification. Frequently, the tentacles are brightly colored, either from the presence of numerous symbiotic algae, the *zooxanthellae*, or from pigments produced by the anemone. The tentacles have specialized stinging cells, the *cnidoblasts*, containing *nematocysts*. The nematocyst is a complex structure, and is employed both for defense and food capture. Upon stimulation, the nematocyst discharges a poisoned dart or an entangling snare. Different types of nematocysts exist, and microscopic examination for the presence of these is often the only way to conclusively identify anemone species, although some authors suggest that the host anemones can be identified simply by inspection.

Classification

All anemones are *coelenterates*, animals with only two layers of cells composing the body, and a single body opening; organs are lacking, or rudimentary; stinging cells (cnidoblasts) are always present. Two body plans, the *medusa*, or jellyfish form and the *polyp*, or flower-animal form, exist among coelenterates. Separation of the three classes of coelenterates is based upon which of these two forms is predominant during the life cycle. In anemones, the polyp stage is the only one present, and these organisms are placed in Class Anthozoa, the "flower animals." Their resemblance to flowers is probably the reason for our long history of interest in anemones as a group.

There are many kinds of anthozoans. Here is a brief outline of

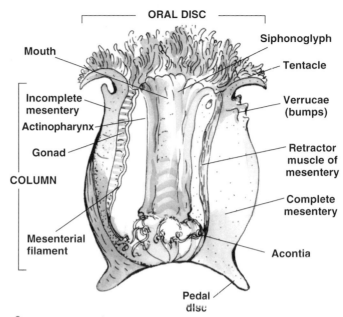

Sea anemone anatomy.

anemone taxonomy. Many related anthozoans are likely to be seen in aquarium stores that also stock anemones.

Subclass Zoantharia: Solitary or colonial anthozoans with tentacles in multiples of six. There are six orders, including the sea mats, stony corals, and false corals, in addition to the anemones.

Order Actinaria: Anemones; solitary anthozoans without skeletal elements.

Tribe Thenaria: Anemones with basilar muscles and a well-defined pedal disc. Within this group, the clownfish host anemones occupy three families:

1. Family Thalassianthidae is exclusively tropical, and includes only one species that hosts clownfishes, *Cryptodendrum adhesivum*. This unusual anemone is host only to Clark's Anemonefishes, *Amphiprion clarkii*. It is very sticky, and has two

Amphiprion clarkii *with* Heteractis malu.

Amphiprion clarkii *with* Heteractis aurora.

Amphiprion clarkii *with* Heteractis crispa.

Amphiprion perideraion *with* Heteractis magnifica.

distinct types of tentacles that are usually of different colors. One type is limited to the outer rim of the oral disc, and is shaped like elongated balloons. The central area of the oral disc is covered with another type of tentacles that look like little gloves. This anemone is not common in the aquarium trade. There are other clownfish hosts that adapt better to captivity, and this species should probably be avoided by hobbyists.

   2. **Family Stichodactylidae** is another exclusively tropical family. The genera *Stichodactyla* and *Heteractis*, the two main host genera for clownfishes, are placed here. *H. aurora*, the Beaded Sea Anemone, is perhaps the easiest of this group to identify, as the tentacles are ribbed with swellings that are often a contrasting color. It hosts seven clownfish species. *H. crispa*, Leathery Sea Anemone, hosts eleven clownfishes. It is sometimes confused with *H. malu*, which in the aquarium trade is usually known as the "Sebae" or "Singapore Sebae" anemone. *H. malu* hosts only *A. clarkii*, a species often incorrectly identified as *A. sebae*. (The true *A. sebae*, a much rarer species, associ-

ates in nature only with *Stichodactyla haddoni*, discussed below.) *H. malu* is most easily recognized by the short tentacles, seldom over an inch (2.5 cm) in length, which are often tipped in magenta. *H. magnifica*, Magnificent Sea Anemone, is also called the "Ritteri Anemone." It is host to ten clownfish species.

Stichodactyla gigantea, the Giant Carpet Anemone of the aquarium trade, is host to seven clownfish species, and can be separated from the other two *Stichodactyla* species by its noticeably longer tentacles, often strikingly colored. *S. haddoni*, Haddon's Sea Anemone, is called the "Saddle Carpet" in the aquarium trade because of the affinity of the Saddleback Clownfish, *A. polymnus*, for this host. The very short tentacles are frequently of two colors, giving the oral disc a mottled appearance. Besides *A. polymnus*, five other clownfish species associate with this anemone. Merten's Sea Anemone is called a Sri Lanka Carpet by aquarium dealers, and is sometimes bright green in color. Its stubby tentacles, shaped like little knobs, are uniform in color, although there may by a contrasting ring of purple pigment encircling the mouth.

Clownfish host anemones in the stichodactylid family have a mixed record of success in the aquarium. The majority of specimens probably die before reaching anything approaching their natural lifespan. *H. magnifica* is especially regarded as difficult, and is known for its habit of wandering all over the aquarium, often being killed or damaged by being sucked into a powerhead or filter intake. It appears that the availability of light, planktonic food, and water movement are important to this species. The fact that it is often beautifully colored, that the most popular clownfish species, *A. ocellaris*, prefers this host, and that it is more commonly

Amphiprion clarkii with Stichodactyla gigantea.

Amphiprion sandaracinos with Stichodactyla mertensi.

Amphiprion polymnus with Stichodactyla haddoni.

Table 6
Summary of Host Anemone Characteristics

Nine species of clownfish host anemones are summarized below, and are listed in order from the hardiest to the most difficult to maintain. Common associations with clownfish species available as tank-reared specimens are included.

Entacmaea quadricolor, Bulb, Bubble-Tip, Maroon, or Rose Anemone. Tentacles inflated at tips, with white band and pink tip (usually). Attaches to hard surface. Naturally hosts Maroon and Bluestripe clownfishes; in the aquarium will also host Common, Tomato, and Clark's clownfishes.

Macrodactyla doreensis, Long Tentacle Anemone, "LTA." Column always red or salmon pink, with verrucae underneath oral disk. Buries column in substrate. Seldom confused. Naturally hosts Clark's and Pink Skunk clownfishes; in the aquarium will also host Maroon, Bluestripe, and Tomato clowns.

Heteractis crispa, Leathery Anemone, Button Anemone. Column tough, leathery, red or yellow in color, and buried in substrate. Tentacles long and pointed. Not common in trade. Hosts Clark's, Bluestripe, True Percula, Pink Skunk, and Saddleback clownfishes.

H. aurora, Beaded Anemone, Aurora Anemone. Not common in the aquarium trade. Buries column in substrate, tentacles with raised, white ridges unmistakable. The only common aquarium clown hosted is Clark's.

H. malu, Sebae Anemone, Singapore Sebae. Column and oral disk uniform pale color, with stubby tentacles usually tipped in magenta. Seldom confused. Hosts only Clark's clownfish in nature, and may host Tomato and Bluestripe clowns in the aquarium.

H. magnifica, Magnificent Anemone, Ritteri Anemone, Red Radianthus Anemone. Seldom mistaken. Attaches to hard surfaces in good current and bright light; in aquariums it may wander. Column smooth, often colorful; tentacles with yellow or white pigment at tips. Hosts Clark's, Bluestripe, Common, Percula, and Pink Skunk clowns.

Carpet Anemones
Stichodactyla gigantea, Giant Carpet Anemone. Tentacles longer than other carpet anemones, and slightly pointed at tips. May be blue, turquoise, or purple in color. Naturally hosts Clark's, Common, and Percula clowns, in the aquarium may host additional species unpredictably.

S. haddoni, Haddon's Carpet, Saddle Carpet Anemone. Tentacles are almost always two colors, imparting a mottled appearance. Naturally hosts Saddleback and Clark's clownfishes; in the aquarium may host additional species unpredictably.

S. mertensi, Merten's Carpet, Sri Lanka Carpet. Tentacles are stubby, knoblike, uniform brown or occasionally bright green in color. Naturally hosts Clark's and Common clownfishes; in the aquarium may host Pink Skunk clown.

46

available than the other hosts for this clown, may explain why many aquarists are tempted to buy this species despite its reputation.

The carpet anemones also pose husbandry problems for the aquarist. All three species require intense lighting, as can be noted from the presence of brightly colored pigments in many specimens. Insufficient light may be one reason for problems. Another problem that may affect all stichodactylid anemones in the aquarium may be incompatibility with other species of coelenterates through nettling.

3. Family Actiniidae is the largest family of anemones, and includes the clownfish host genera *Entacmaea* and *Macrodactyla*, the tropical Florida genus *Condylactis*, and most of the common, larger anemones of temperate waters. Hardiness is a characteristic, relatively speaking, for the two actiniid anemones that host clownfishes. These are *Macrodactyla doreensis* and *Entacmaea quadricolor*. *Macrodactyla* is known as Long Tentacle Anemone, often abbreviated simply as "LTA." The red column topped with bluish-gray verrucae is distinctive, although usually the column will be buried in the substrate. The long tentacles, gray, bluish, or pinkish in color, often twist into a spiral shape. It hosts only three clownfish species, but in the aquarium is accepted by additional ones. It is reasonably hardy but does need a soft, sandy substrate in which to bury the column. Lacking this it will wander around, fail to attach, and eventually die.

Entacmaea quadricolor, called the Bulb Anemone in the aquarium trade, holds the record for clownfish species hosted, at 13. The tips of the tentacles look like the nipple on an old-fashioned glass baby bottle. No other anemone has this feature. There are two types of *Entacmaea*, a fact that may have important implications for aquarium care. In shallow water, a "clonal form" occurs in large aggregations. In deep water, the polyps are of the "solitary form" and can be over a foot across. Despite the fact that the two different types may arise as a result of differing environmental conditions at different depths, it appears that the clonal form reproduces readily by asexual reproduction, whereas the solitary form reproduces sexually. Vegetative reproduction of the clonal form in the aquarium has been reported by several aquarists.

Entacmaea is called the Maroon Anemone by some aquarium wholesalers, as a result of its long-recognized association with the Maroon Clownfish, *Premnas biaculeatus*. A rare color variety, in which the body is red with pink tentacles, is called Rose Anemone by aquarium dealers, and commands a high price.

Anemone Conservation Issues

Whether the clownfish host anemones should be collected in large numbers should be given consideration. In the first place, survival of larvae to become adult anemones is thought to be a rare occurrence; very few small individuals of any anemone species are observed in the field. Further, a low larval survival rate is characteristic of species that are long-lived. There are documented instances of captive anemones living to be quite old. Larger anemones observed on coral reefs are almost certainly over a century old. That such long-lived creatures often survive only a few months in captivity is strong evidence that aquarium hobbyists should become more adept at keeping them, or should avoid them altogether in favor of species more likely to live out a natural lifespan in captivity.

I recommend that aquarium hobbyists select only *Entacmaea* and *Macrodactyla* as the clownfish hosts of

Premnas biaculeatus *(Sumatra form).*

Amphiprion polymnys sulanesi.

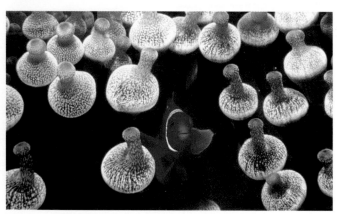

Premnas biaculeatus *with* Entacmaea quadricolor *(Note the distinctive shape of the anemone's tentacles.)*

primary interest, and avoid the more difficult species. *Entacmaea* seems to me to be the most appropriate aquarium species. It is the most abundant host anemone in nature, it is widely distributed, occurring from the Red Sea to Samoa, it is host to many species of clownfishes, and it has a potential for captive propagation through vegetative reproduction. In my experience, it settles into the aquarium readily and does not, in contrast to *Macrodactyla*, require substrate into which to bury the column, preferring instead to attach to a rock or other solid object. This species clearly deserves more attention from aquarists.

Tankmates for Clownfishes and Anemones

Compatible Fish Species

For aquarium purposes, clownfish habitats can be lumped into a few simplistic categories. Lagoons, which can often be collected by wading at low tide, are more commonly the source of specimens than are deeper waters. Clownfish distribution is determined by the habitat preferences of the host anemones. Consequently, the assortment of additional species that may be found near a group of clownfishes is often characteristic for that habitat. It can be useful to describe typical communities to create a set of guidelines as a starting point.

Biotopes

A biotope is a small area within an ecosystem that is usually defined in terms of a characteristic community of organisms that are found together because their ecologies interact. In terrestrial environments, plants often determine the character of a specific biotope, while in coral reef habitats, photosynthetic invertebrates may play a similar role. The geographic distribution of clownfishes is determined to some extent by the distribution of appropriate host anemones, for example. Exercise your creativity in designing a natural biotope for the clownfish of your selection, and choose as tankmates specimens that appeal to you.

Specimens for the Marine Tank

Among the most widely available specimens for the marine tank are the soft corals, sea mats, disc anemones, and large-polyped scleractinian (LPS) corals that inhabit shallow, inshore waters. Rapidly gaining favor among aquarium enthusiasts are the small-polyped scleractinian (SPS) corals. However, the ability of coelenterates to engage in chemical warfare with each other, often in the absence of direct physical contact, has obvious implications to the specialist interested in clownfish host anemones. Clownfish hosts should be given separate aquariums from other coelenterates, unless one is absolutely certain that no negative interactions will occur. Unfortunately, this must often be determined by direct observation. Accordingly, I have made no recommendations for combining clownfish host anemones with other species of coelenterates.

For the smaller system described earlier (page 35), I suggested exhibiting *Amphiprion ocellaris* without its host anemone in a lagoon habitat simulation. This habitat would also be home to the Mandarin Fish, *Pterosynchiropus splendidus*, or its cousin, the Spotted Mandarin, *Synchiropus picturatus*. One of these could be accommodated along with the pair of clownfishes in a 30-gallon (114 L) aquarium.

Pterosynchiropus splendidus.

Nemateleotris magnifica.

Nemateleotris decora.

Pseudochromis porphyreus.

Pseudochromis paccagnellae.

Pseudochromis diadema.

Pseudocheilinus tetrataenia.

Gobiodon okinawae.

Oxycirrhites typus.

Avoid keeping host anemones with other coelenterates.

   Long regarded as inappropriate choices for the novice aquarist, these two dragonets are remarkably easy to maintain when their needs are understood. Seldom subject to problems unrelated to their feeding habits, many dragonets starve in captivity because they feed only on tiny crustaceans and rarely accept any substitute for this diet. However, an aquarium containing live rock, if properly maintained, develops a thriving population of these organisms after it has been up and running for about eight months to a year. Copepods, a primary source of food for the dragonet, may be observed as barely visible white dots that scurry among piles of debris or algal mats on the rocks. When a dragonet is introduced into such an aquarium, it has access to a supply of natural food. Make sure each dragonet has at least 30 gallons (114 L) of tank capacity, in a natural system with one pound of live rock per gallon. Specimens have thrived for several years under these conditions. Hobbyists are cautioned to look carefully at any specimen for signs of starvation. If the dragonet is held

Dendrochirus brachypterus.

Centropyge bispinosus.

Centropyge bicolor.

under conditions that prevent its access to appropriate foods, it will lose weight and become noticeably concave in the belly region, and in the area just behind the eyes, in front of the dorsal fin. Specimens in an emaciated state require special attention if they are to recover, and are not recommended to the average hobbyist.

Invertebrates from the lagoon should also be added, if only to help to keep the tank in good condition. It is easier to work in the lagoon than in deeper water, and SCUBA equipment is not often available to collectors in the developing countries that supply marine aquarium specimens. Thus, invertebrates, fishes and anemones from this habitat are widely available.

Another example mentioned (page 41) was an aquarium with *Entacmaea quadricolor* and *Amphiprion melanopus* that might be found on a reef top or in a deeper area of the lagoon. I suggest including only one anemone to leave room for its progeny, with five juvenile clowns. Dartfishes, such as the Common Firefish, *Nemateleotris magnifica*, and the Purple Firefish, *N. decora*, occur here in pairs. The striking Purple Dottyback, *Pseudochromis porphyreus*, is often very common in this habitat, hovering just above the coral. Many other *Pseudochromis* are now being propagated in hatcheries. As described below, *Tridacna maxima* and two shrimps, *Lysmata amboiensis* and *L. debelius*, would also be at home in this aquarium. A Neon Wrasse, *Pseudocheilinus hexataenia*, will help to protect the giant clams from parasitic snails they may be harboring. A coral goby, such as *Gobiodon citrinus*, might also be included in this tank, or the Longnose Hawkfish, *Oxycirrhites typus*. I suggest limiting the total number of fish (in the 1 to 3 inch [2.5–7.6 cm] size range) to no more than one per 10 gallons (38 L).

Because they are mobile, fishes are not as restricted in their habitat preferences as are sessile invertebrates. Wide-ranging aquarium fishes may be found in a variety of habitats both shoreward and seaward of the reef. Some good companions for clownfish might include:
• Fuzzy Dwarf Lionfish, *Dendrochirus brachypterus*
• Coral Beauty Dwarf Angel, *Centropyge bispinossus*
• Bicolor Dwarf Angel, *Centropyge bicolor*
• Herald's Dwarf Angel, *Centropyge heraldi*
• Bicolor Blenny, *Escenius bicolor*
• Canary Blenny, *Meiacanthus ovalauensis*

Do not include the lionfish with a clownfish small enough to be swallowed, even though these fishes usually feed on crustaceans (which obviously rules out including them with shrimps or small crabs).

Compatible Invertebrates

Giant Clams

Several species of giant clams might be found in either the lagoon or the reef top habitats. *Tridacna squamosa* would be the most likely choice from the lagoon, since it prefers sheltered shallows. *T. gigas*, *T. crocea*, and *T. maxima* would also be appropriate. *T. gigas* and *T. crocea* are typically attached to a hard surface. The latter species frequently bores into coral heads, for example.

Outer reefs are the home of the most common giant clam, *T. derasa*, which is also an adaptable species that can be recommended. Hatchery-raised giant clams are the only ones available, as overharvesting has led to protection of wild clam populations.

The mantle of the giant clam is filled with zooxanthellae, symbiotic algae that live in the tissues of the clam and carry

Centropyge heraldi.

Meiacanthus ovalauensis.

out photosynthesis. Similar organisms live symbiotically with clownfish host sea anemones; hence, conditions suitable for the anemones are also suitable for giant clams. Coloration of the mantle ranges from bright green to blue and purple. Each individual clam looks a little different from every other one, and all are quite beautiful.

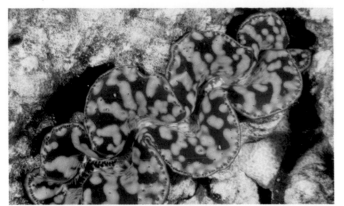

Tridacna squamosa.

Tridacna gigas.

Tridacna crocea.

Care. The care of all species of giant clams is the same. The clam relies exclusively upon its zooxanthellae for food. It absorbs both inorganic and organic nutrients from the water, probably for the primary benefit of the zooxanthellae. Such nutrients include phosphate, ammonia, and nitrate; thus, *Tridacna* actually helps to maintain low levels of nitrate and phosphate in its aquarium. Clams also require ample oxygen, a high, stable pH, and high-intensity lighting. Clams also need protection from irritants and parasites. *Aiptasia* (harbor anemones) can be troublesome, as can small snails. The latter can be controlled, as mentioned above, by keeping a Neon Wrasse in the tank, although this fish is not often seen in the lagoon.

Sponges

Many species of sponges that are collected for the aquarium do best in shady locations, as they are easily "swamped" if algae growth gets started on them. Sponges have a porous body, and it is through the pores that they feed and acquire oxygen. Water circulates through the sponge and microscopic food particles are captured. If algae or detritus are allowed to accumulate, clogging the pores, the sponge will suffocate and die. Various species of sponges are imported from both the Indo-Pacific and Caribbean regions.

Care. Never allow detritus or algae to accumulate on the surface of the sponge. Supply water movement to aid the sponge in feeding. Sponges feed on very small particles, and possibly absorb dissolved organic materials, such as proteins, from the water. In my experience, sponges do well in the aquarium, if these simple requirements are met. Several kinds may grow voluntarily on the aquarium decor and glass, after the aquarium has been in operation for a while.

Aiptasia *anemones colonizing a dead coral skeleton.*

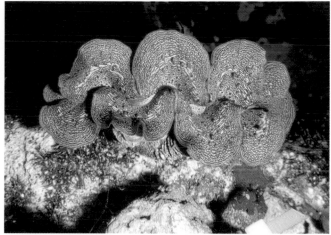

Tridacna maxima.

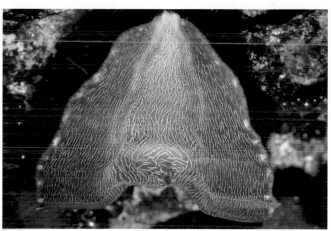

Tridacna derasa.

Unidentified orange sponge from Maldives.

The ability of some sponges to reproduce vegetatively is legendary; a standard college biology lab demonstration involves chopping up a living sponge in a blender, placing the puree in an appropriate environment, and observing how the sponge reaggregates itself and regenerates over the next few weeks. Only certain species of sponges respond favorably to the procedure, however.

Sabellastarte sanctijosephi.

Sabellastarte indica.

Tubeworms

All of the commonly available tube-worms can be included in the clownfish tank. Available species include *Sabellastarte sanctijosephi*, which comes from Hawaii, and *Spirobranchus giganteus*, which is found on reefs throughout the world. Various other tubeworms, including *Sabella melanostigma, S. elegans, Spirographis, Spirobranchus tetraceros*, and many more, are either imported individually, or can be found on live rock specimens.

Care. All tubeworms are very easily kept, and need no special feeding. In my experience, *Sabella melanostigma* reproduces itself readily. I have seen this worm growing in lovely colonies in many hobbyists' tanks.

Echinoderms

Nearly all echinoderms prefer at least a shady spot in which to retreat from time to time. Brittlestars and serpent stars (Class Ophiuroidea) feed on stray bits of this and that, which they locate during their nocturnal excursions around the tank. The available species are largely from Florida, and are only occasionally imported from the Indo-Pacific. Since they are all useful scavengers, they should be included in the clownfish tank. Feather stars (Class Crinoidea), on the other hand, and the similar but distantly related basket stars (Class Ophiuroidea), are much more fragile. These specimens are not to be recommended as aquarium specimens.

With some exceptions, "regular" starfish (Class Asteroidea) are to be avoided in a tank that also includes sessile invertebrates such as giant clams, as they have the habit of eating anything and everything. The exceptions, however, make attractive additions. These include two species of *Fromia*, the Little Red Starfish, *F. elegans*, and the Orange Tile Starfish, *F. monilis*.

Fromia monilis.

A delicate crinoid, or feather star.

Sea urchins (Class Echinoidea) are vegetarians, and are sometimes placed in the aquarium for algae control. However, only urchins smaller than a golf ball are recommended, and these should be replaced as they grow. Larger ones may feed too heavily, or may topple rocks as they move about the tank. Urchins generally are found in shallower waters where their food source occurs.

Sea cucumbers (Class Holothuroidea) are either burrowers or filter feeders. An especially attractive genus are the Sea Apples, *Pseudocolochirus,* of which there are two or three species or color types imported for the aquarium. Sea Apples are conspicuously colored, advertising to potential predators that their flesh is toxic. Their eggs have been called "poisonous candy" for fishes by Sprung and Delbeek (1994, see Useful Literature and Addresses, page 65). Aquarists should be aware of potential problems that these organisms can pose for fish housed in the same aquarium. Otherwise, Sea Apples are interesting animals, and can be long-lived in the aquarium if adequately fed. Other species of filter-feeding cucumbers appear in shipments from time to time. Some of them are quite colorful.

Care. These cucumbers will slowly starve if food is insufficient. The telltale sign of inadequate feeding is a reduction in the size of the animal. If this occurs, add a commercial food product designed for filter feeders once or twice a week, and observe the animal for signs of renewed growth. Burrowing cucumbers feed the same

A sea urchin.

Lybia, *the Pom-Pom Crab.*

way as earthworms, ingesting the substrate and digesting the edible matter therein. Most are found where rich sediments abound, as in grass beds. Inclusion of a few specimens will help to keep the substrate "cultivated." Most burrowing cucumbers available come from Florida.

Snails

I suggest that anyone interested in snails should purchase a good seashell identification book and learn to recognize the species. Accurate

Neopterolisthes maculatus.

58

identification is of utmost importance with mollusks, since their habits and diets vary widely. I have seen harmless species displayed side by side with predatory types in dealers' tanks.

Herbivorous grazing snails, from the trochid and turbinid families are frequently imported for algae control. These are now almost universally included in all types of marine aquarium displays. At the other extreme are snails, such as nudibranchs, which are so rigidly specialized in their feeding habits that they are impossible to maintain in a home aquarium. In between are a host of others, including some that would make beautiful, intriguing aquarium subjects for the hobbyist willing to do the background work.

More likely, however, the only snails you will keep will be for algae control. Several species of *Turbo* snails, along with *Astraea tecta*, all collected from North American shores, are sold by aquarium dealers. An appropriate number should be included in your clownfish aquarium. I prefer *Astraea* for its size, hardiness, and efficient algae removal.

Crustaceans

Although the crustacean group is one of the most diverse and abundant in the sea, relatively few species are suitable for the clownfish aquarium. Among the most useful are several species of small hermit crabs that are collected in Florida. Hermit crabs lack protective integument on the posterior portion of their bodies, and borrow an empty snail shell for protection. *Clibanarius tricolor*, the Blue-Leg Hermit Crab, and *Paguristes cadenanti*, the Scarlet Hermit Crab, are prized for their algae removal abilities. Although not as useful in this regard, other small hermits, including *Calcinus tibicen*, *Pylopagurus operculatus*, and *Aniculus strigatus* are seen from time to time. Larger hermit crabs are often aggressive and destructive; you should therefore avoid hermit crabs that occupy a shell much larger than an English walnut.

Another useful species from Florida is the Green Sculptured Coral Crab, *Mithrax sculptus*. It is the color of seaweed, and has spoon-shaped tips on its major claws. Otherwise, it resembles familiar edible crabs, although it is much smaller, about the size of a quarter. Somewhat secretive, it is included in the aquarium for algae control. Most other true crabs are far too aggressive to make good tankmates for clownfishes. An interesting exception is the Pom Pom Crab, *Lybia*, which has the amusing habit of carrying two small anemones in its claws. These are brandished as weapons, as well as being put to use as mops to collect detritus upon which the crab feeds. Anemone crabs, such as *Neopterollsthes maculatus*, live in symbiotic association with anemones, including clownfish hosts. Sometimes the crab's presence will be tolerated by a resident clownfish, and sometimes not. Best results are to be had by allowing the crab to become established in the anemone for a week or two, and then adding juvenile clowns. Peaceful cohabitation is not guaranteed, however.

The following shrimps are excellent companions for clownfishes and other compatible invertebrates: the Florida Peppermint Shrimp, *Lysmata wurde-*

Lysmata amboiensis.

manni, the Scarlet Cleaner Shrimp, *Lysmata amboiensis*, and the Fire Shrimp, *Lysmata debelius*. The latter two species may exhibit cleaning behavior, in which the crustacean is actually approached by fishes seeking removal of ectoparasites. The shrimps move about the fish's body, removing parasites and dead tissues. They supplement their diet with these tidbits, although other foods are taken when the cleaning business is slow. The Florida Peppermint Shrimp is useful in controlling small anemones *(Aiptasia)* that may reproduce overabundantly if left unchecked. It is harmless to the clownfish host anemones.

Breeding Clownfishes

If one places a breeding pair of clownfishes into a naturalistic habitat aquarium, as described in this book, one is likely to be rewarded with a spawning. In my experience, when a mature pair has lived in the aquarium about a year, and has received a good diet and otherwise proper husbandry, the pair will spawn without further encouragement from the hobbyist, and will, in general, exhibit its natural pattern of reproductive behavior, spawning every few weeks for a while and then taking a "rest period" before spawning resumes. The aquarist who owns such a pair of clownfishes will have the opportunity to observe the ritualized courtship behavior that precedes spawning, as well as the spawning event itself. The pair will then tend the eggs, not unlike the familiar freshwater angelfish, fanning them and removing debris, until hatching. I have seen all of this take place even in unlikely situations, such as in a dealer's community display aquarium.

The Spawning Aquarium

While the larger the aquarium, the better, clownfishes will spawn in aquariums as small as 30 gallons (114 L), and under conditions that are anything but naturalistic. In commercial operations that I have observed, the eggs are usually deposited on a plastic plate that is removed from the spawning aquarium to a rearing tank. No effort is made to duplicate the clownfish's native habitat, and no anemone is provided. Given this propensity to spawn, it is not surprising that, given a mature pair and a natural tank, obtaining fertilized eggs is not a problem.

Rearing the Larvae

Obtaining a suitable breeding pair does not present a problem, either, as can easily be understood from the discussion of gender determination and pair formation on page 6. So why doesn't every hobbyist with an interest in clownfishes spawn and rear his or her own specimens? The problem lies in rearing the larvae.

Although the parents will care for a brood of eggs, carefully aerating and cleaning them and driving off predators, when the eggs finally hatch they are likely to eat every one. At hatching, clownfishes, like most marine fishes, are hardly more than a mobile brain and a pair of eyes. For several days after leaving the egg, the larvae live off stored nutrients from their yolk sacs. Instinctively swimming near the surface, they spend about 8 to 12 days as part of the plankton, feeding on smaller organisms and in turn becoming prey for an assortment of microscopic predators. The relatively short larval phase, as compared to many other marine species including other members of the damselfish family, results in several species' inhabiting a limited range. The larval clownfishes are not at the mercy of ocean currents for a sufficiently long period to be carried far from their parents' reef tract.

Adequately duplicating the larval habitat and, in particular, providing sufficient food of an appropriate kind is the primary obstacle to the culture of clownfishes, and, indeed, of any marine fish species so far successfully spawned in captivity.

This chapter is not meant to be a guide for those who aspire to start a business venture raising clownfishes. What I hope to do is encourage the serious amateur with enthusiasm to be set up for a challenge—and the time and space to pursue it—on a path that will have a reasonable likelihood of successful rearing of a few specimens from an occasional spawn. My advice is based on reports from rank amateurs working with minimal equipment, as well as the proprietors of large-scale commercial operations.

A mated pair of Amphiprion ocellaris. *The female is on the right.*

Broodstock

If you establish an aquarium with a pair or family grouping of clownfishes according to the suggestions in previous chapters, you will very likely obtain a spawn. The fishes characteristically locate the nest on a rock near their anemone, often protected by the anemone's tentacles. If you observe your fishes cleaning a hard surface within their territory, this is the most likely spawning site. If you intend to rear the larvae, it is essential that they be separated from the parents, either immediately upon hatching (which usually occurs just past dusk about a week after spawning), or for the entire incubation process (trickier, but likely to save a larger percentage of the spawn). If the parents are the only fishes in the display aquarium, it may be relatively simple to remove them just prior to hatching, after leaving the duties of egg incubation and care to their expert attention.

Wild-Caught Pairs

If the ultimate goal is breeding, you should pay some attention to the selection of the parents. For some species not presently in hatchery production, a wild-caught pair may be the only choice. The disadvantages to selecting a wild pair are twofold. First, clownfishes often arrive in poor condition and must receive proper quarantine, and often treatment for a disease condition, prior to retail sale. This, coupled with the obvious requirement that everyone from the collector to the retailer must keep the pair together and keep track of them (often among thousands of other specimens) entails more work than would be the case for many other marine fishes. Wild pairs, therefore, are rather costly. Second, with a wild pair there is no way to know how old the fishes might be or how often they have spawned in the past. You might end up paying top dollar for two fishes nearing the end of their lives.

Inbreeding

On the other hand, a problem with choosing tank-raised clownfishes as broodstock is inbreeding. If possible, two parents should never be chosen from the same hatchery, because this increases the likelihood of breeding two siblings. Spawns from closely related parents may have a lower survival rate, and, in any case, inbreeding is considered detrimental to the vigor of any domestic line of any species. Another way to avoid inbreeding is to mate captive-produced stock with a wild counterpart.

Apart from careful selection of the potential parents, your chances of successfully spawning a pair of clowns depends largely upon their state of health. Vigorous specimens will result from careful attention to aquarium maintenance, and a fresh, varied diet including, for at least one species *(A. perideraion),* filamentous algae. (I have observed several other species of clownfishes feeding on algae in the aquarium.) Tiny crustaceans and invertebrate larvae, planktonic organisms snatched from the water column, are important food sources for clownfishes on the reef. In the aquarium, virtually any of the available small, meaty seafoods, including brine shrimp, mysids, chopped seafoods, and even flake foods, are usually accepted.

Food Cultures

As previously indicated, feeding larval clownfishes is not so straightforward. The key to success in rearing them is having a continuous supply of

150 microns

Brachionus.

living food constantly available to the larvae from the time they lose the yolk sac until they are large enough to take brine shrimp nauplii. Although fish breeders are constantly experimenting with a wide array of plankton substitutes as larval foods, the tried-and-true first food for clownfishes remains the rotifer, *Brachionus.* This tiny invertebrate, barely visible to the naked eye, feeds on unicellular algae.

System Design

Since larval food culture is critical to success in rearing larval clownfishes, establishing an efficient system for this purpose should be your first consideration. Complete instructions for establishing a culture system can be found in Moe, 1982 (see Useful Literature and Addresses, page 65). An illustration of Moe's system accompanies this chapter.

If you choose to use the display aquarium as a breeding tank, or perhaps if the resident clownfishes make this choice for you, this will probably provide all the eggs and larvae you can handle. If you plan on attempting more intensive production, you will probably want separate breeding tanks for each pair.

In any event, you will need a larval rearing tank. Here again, precise instructions can be found in Moe, 1982.

Hobbyists have reported greatest success with a rounded container, which prevents the larval fish from congregating in corners. Restricting illumination of the container, by means of a black plastic shroud, for example, is necessary. Excessive light can actually harm the larvae. Gentle aeration of the rearing tank provides oxygen and helps to keep food organisms in suspension. Partial water changes must be carried out daily, with siphoning of debris off the bottom of the rearing tank. Should transfer of the larvae

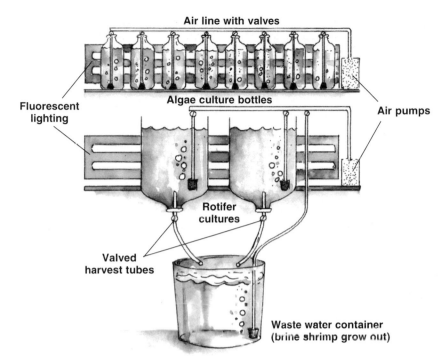

Air line with valves

Algae culture bottles

Fluorescent
lighting

Air pumps

Rotifer
cultures

Valved
harvest tubes

Waste water container
(brine shrimp grow out)

Food culture system for marine fish larvae.

from one container to another become necessary, they should be dipped up carefully using a cup or ladle, in order to avoid damaging them with a net, bulb baster, or similar tool.

My purpose here is to give you the most basic information about marine fish breeding. You can decide for yourself if this aspect of the hobby is for you.

Finally, many first-time fish breeders (including those in the freshwater hobby) make the mistake of failing to provide sufficient grow-out space for their juvenile fish. A single spawn can consist of 100 to 1,000 eggs. If your pair produces 500 eggs, and you are successful in rearing 10 percent of them through metamorphosis, you will need accommodations for 50 one-inch (2.5 cm) fish.

The accompanying illustrations depict two designs for multiple tank-rearing systems similar to those employed by commercial fish breeders.

Time Frame for Hatching

From spawning to hatching, clown-fish eggs require six to seven days. Hatching usually occurs at dusk.

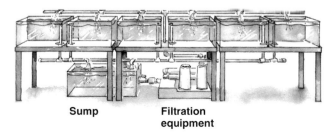

Sump   Filtration
              equipment

Multiple-tank system on a bench.

63

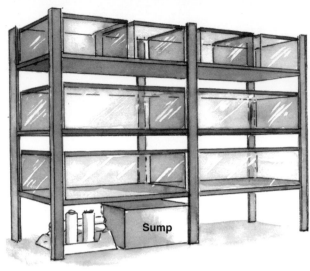

Filtration equipment

Multiple tank system on a rack.

good water quality, and an adequate diet, care similar in all respects to that recommended elsewhere in this book, the immature clownfishes should be capable of spawning by the time they are a year old.

Summary

From the foregoing it should be apparent that spawning and rearing clownfishes take some effort. Fortunately, more and more hobbyists who attempt to breed marine fishes at home are achieving success, and this aspect of the hobby is gaining popularity all the time. If you live in a small apartment, you may have to be content with watching your pair of clowns going through their interesting courtship, spawning, and parental behavior. On the other hand, with a modest amount of equipment, anyone can raise a few clownfishes in a spare corner of the garage. Hobbyists across America have told me that becoming a successful marine fish breeder is the ultimate reward for participation in the aquarium hobby. If breeding marine fishes strikes your fancy, the Breeders Registry, an organization dedicated to the captive propagation of marine fishes, welcomes participation by both amateurs and professionals alike (see Useful Literature and Addresses, page 65).

The larvae remain planktonic for about 8 to 12 days, the crucial period during which they must receive rotifers. When the larvae metamorphose into recognizable copies of their parents, and begin to take larger foods such as newly hatched brine shrimp, most of the difficulties associated with rearing them are past. If provided with sufficient space,

Useful Literature and Addresses

Helpful Reading

Adey, Walter H. and Karen Loveland. *Dynamic Aquaria*. New York: Academic Press, 1991.

Allen, Gerald R. *The Anemonefishes of the World; Species, Care and Breeding*. Mentor, Ohio: Aquariums Systems, 1980.

Barnes, R.D. *Invertebrate Zoology*. 3rd ed. Philadelphia, Pennsylvania: W.B. Saunders, 1974.

Bearman, Gerry, ed. *Seawater, Its Composition, Properties, and Behaviour*. New York: Pergamon Press, 1989.

Blasiola, G.C. Description, preliminary studies, and probable etiology of head and lateral line erosion (HLLE) in the palette tang (*Paracanthurus hepatus*) and other Acanthurids. *Proceedings of the Second International Congress of Aquariology*, Musee Oceanographique, Monaco, as abstracted in *Seascope 5*, Summer, 1988.

Bold, H.C. and M.J. Wynne *Introduction to the Algae*. Inglewood Cliffs, New Jersey: Prentice Hall, 1978.

Committee on Marine Invertebrates, Institute of Laboratory Animal Resources, Assembly of Life Sciences, National Research Council (1981) *Laboratory Animal Management: Marine Invertebrates*. Washington, DC: National Academy Press, 382 pp.

Debelius, Helmut. *Fishes for the Invertebrate Aquarium*. Mentor, Ohio: Aquarium Systems, 1989.

Delbeek, J.C. and J. Sprung *The Reef Aquarium, Volume I*. Coconut Grove, Florida: Ricordea Publishing, 1994.

Dunn, Daphne Fautin (1981) *The Clownfish Sea Anemones: Stichodactylidae (Coelenterate:Actinaria) and Other Sea Anemones Symbiotic with Pomacentrid Fishes*. Transactions of the American Philosophical Society *71(1)* : 15–28.

Fautin, Daphne and Gerald Allen. *Field Guide to Anemonefishes and Their Host Sea Anemones*. Perth, Australia: Western Australian Museum, 1986.

Goldstein, Robert J. *Marine Reef Aquarium Handbook*. Hauppauge, New York: Barron's Educational Series, 1997.

Hall, K. and D.R. Bellwood. (1995) Histological effects of cyanide, stress, and starvation on the intestinal mucosa of *Pomacentrus coelestis*, a marine aquarium fish species. *Journal of Fish Biology* 47: 438–454.

Haywood, Martyn, and Sue Wells. *The Manual of Marine Invertebrates*. Morris Plains, New Jersey: Tetra Press, 1989.

Heslinga, G., T.C. Watson, and T. Isama. *Giant Clam Farming*. Honolulu, Hawaii: Pacific Fisheries Development Foundation (NMFS/NOAA), 1990.

Larson, R.J. and J.W. Cooper, "Phylum Cnidaria," in Walls, J.G., ed. *Encyclopedia of Marine Invertebrates*. Neptune City, New Jersey: TFH Publications, 1982.

Magruder, William H. and Jeffrey W. Hunt. *Seaweeds of Hawaii*.

Honolulu, Hawaii: Oriental Publishing Company, 1979.

McLanahan, J. (1973) Growth media—marine. *In Handbook of Phycological Methods*, J.R. Stein, ed. Cambridge University Press, Cambridge, England. pp. 25–51.

Moe, Martin A., Jr. *The Marine Aquariums Handbook. Beginner to Breeder.* Plantation, Florida: Green Turtle Publications, 1982.

_____. *The Marine Aquarium Reference. Systems and Invertebrates.* Plantation, Florida: Green Turtle Publications, 1989.

_____. *Breeding the Orchid Dottyback. An Aquarist's Journal.* Plantation, Florida: Green Turtle Publications, 1997.

Morris, Percy A. *A Field Guide to Shells.* Boston, Massachusetts: Houghton-Miflin Company, 1973.

Myers, Robert F. *Micronesian Reef Fishes.* Guam: Coral Graphics, 1989.

Nostrapour, Fernando (1997) "Is the White-Bonnet Anemonefish (*Amphiprion leucocranos*) a Hybrid? *Aquarium Frontiers.* March/April 1997.

Paletta, Michael (1993) "Anemone Propagation." *SeaScope 10 (2)* Winter 1993.

Roessler, Carl. *The Underwater Wilderness. Life Around the Great Reefs.* New York: McGraw-Hill, 1986.

Smith, Deboyd L. *A Guide to Marine Coastal Plankton and Marine Invertebrate Larvae.* Dubuque, Iowa: Kendall-Hunt Publishing Company, 1977.

Spotte, Stephen. *Seawater Aquariums.* New York: John Wiley & Sons, 1979.

_____. *Captive Seawater Fishes.* New York: John Wiley & Sons, 1992.

Sprung, Julian and Charles Delbeek. *The Reef Aquarium, Volume Two.* Coconut Grove, Florida: Ricordea Publishing, Inc., 1997.

Steene, Roger C. *Coral Reefs: Nature's Richest Realm.* Bathurst, NSW, Australia: Crawford House Press, 1990.

Taylor, W. Randolph *Marine Algae of the Tropical and Subtropical Coasts of the Americas.* Ann Arbor, Michigan: University of Michigan Press, 1960.

Tullock, John. *Natural Reef Aquariums.* Shelburne, Vermont: Microcosm, 1997.

_____. *Your First Marine Aquarium.* Hauppauge, New York: Barron's Educational Series, 1998.

Periodicals

Aquarium Fish
P.O. Box 6050
Mission Viejo, CA 92690
www.aquariumfish.com

Freshwater and Marine Aquarium
144 W. Sierra Madre Blvd.
Sierra Madre, CA 91024
800-523-1736
www.mag-web.com/fama

Marine Fish Monthly
3273 US Hwy 61 East
Luttrell, TN 37779
800-937-3963
email: bphipps503@aol.com

Tropical Fish Hobbyist
One TFH Plaza
Neptune City, NJ 07753
732-988-8400
www.tropical.fish.hobbyist.net

Hobbyists with a computer may also enjoy Aquarium Frontiers Online (www.aquariumfrontiers.com), as well as PetPath (www.petpath.com), an online service from Time, Inc.

Hobbyists interested in breeding marine fish should visit the Breeder's Registry, at http://breeders-registry.gen.ca.us

Selected Sources

Listed below are sources for some of the fish, invertebrates, and equipment mentioned in this book.

Clownfish, Anemones, and Other Live Specimens

Aquatic Specialists
3721 North Broadway
Knoxville, TN 37917
423-687-2704
www.aquatic-specialists.com
Ships live marine specimens directly to hobbyists nationwide.

C-Quest
P.O. Box 1163
Salinas, PR 00751
809-845-3909
www.c-quest.com
Hatchery produces clownfish, dottybacks, and other marine fish. Wholesale only.

Sea Critters
13005 Sea Critter Lane
Dover, FL 33527
813-986-6521

Anclote Aquaculture
c/o Tom Frakes
Aquarium Systems, Inc.
8141 Tyler Blvd.
Mentor, OH 44060

Oceans, Reefs, and Aquariums
5600 U.S. 1 North, ACTED Bldg.
Ft. Pierce, FL 34946
561-468-7008

Inland Aquatics
10 Ohio St.
Terre Haute, IN 47807
812-232-9000
email: NLandAqua@aol.com

Aquatic Wildlife Company
5200 N. Lee Highway
Cleveland, TN 37312
423-559-9000
www.aquaticwildlife.com

Indo-Pacific Sea Farms
73-4460 Queens Hwy., #107
Kailua-Kona, HI 96740
808-334-1709

Additional sources may be located by visiting the web site of the American Marinelife Dealers Association at www.execpc.com/~jkos/amda.

Equipment and Supplies

Many of the sources listed below are wholesale only. Individuals are encouraged to visit a local retailer to obtain these products.

Approximately 100 dealer listings may be found on the American Marinelife Dealers Association web site at www.execpc.com/~jkos/amda.

Aquaculture Supply
33418 Old St. Joe Road
Dade City, FL 33525
352-567-8540
www.aquaculture-supply.com
Live food cultures, culture information, laboratory and aquaculture equipment of all types. Catalog $6.00.

Aquarium Systems
8141 Tyler Blvd.
Mentor, OH 44060
800-822-1100
www.aquariumsystems.com
Manufactures a variety of aquarium equipment and supplies, including test kits, salt mix, and filtration products.

A pair of clownfish nestles in an Entacmaea *anemone.*

Champion Lighting and Supply
818 Pleasant Ave.
Wyndmoor, PA 19038
800-673-7822
www.championlighting.com
    Retail/wholesale. Extensive line of aquarium equipment, including precision dosing pumps.

Energy Savers Unlimited, Inc.
910 E. Sandhill Ave.
Carson, CA 90746
800-678-8844
www.esuweb.com
    Aquarium equipment, especially lighting systems. Wholesale only.

Perfecto Manufacturing, Inc.
P.O. Box 539
Noblesville, IN 46060
888-773-6627
    Wholesale only. High-quality aquarium tanks.

Spectrapure, Inc.
738 S. Perry Lane
Tempe, AZ 85281
800-685-2783
    Water purification equipment, including RO and DI systems. Wholesale only.

That Fish Place
237 Centerville Road
Lancaster, PA 17603
888-842-8738
www.thatpetplace.com
    Retail mail order source for all types of aquarium equipment and supplies. Does not ship live fish or invertebrates.

West Coast Aquatics
906 Calle Colorado
Thousand Oaks, CA 91360
    Aquarium equipment, particularly high-efficiency fluid chillers. Wholesale only.

Glossary

Alkalinity: The resistance of a solution to a change in pH as acid is added. (Synonyms: carbonate hardness, KH, alkali reserve)

Amphipod: Any of several species of crustaceans, usually smaller than ¼" in length, distinguished by a laterally compressed body. They are an important component of a healthy aquarium's microfauna.

Amyloodinium: A dinoflagellate fish parasite that often causes death in marine aquarium fish.

Biodiversity: The measure of species richness for a given ecosystem. Systems with many species in a geographically limited area are said to have high biodiversity.

Biotope: A community of organisms characteristic of a specific habitat.

Brooklynella: A ciliated protozoan skin parasite common on clownfishes that have been subjected to stressful or unsanitary conditions.

Calcification: Extraction of calcium (Ca^{2+}) ions from seawater by any of several types of organisms, including stony corals, echinoderms, and crustaceans.

Copepod: Any of several species of crustaceans, usually just visible to the naked eye, characterized by microscopic anatomical details. They are an important component of a healthy aquarium's microfauna.

Coral reef: A massive underwater structure comprised of the skeletons of living coral polyps, together with associated organisms, including seaweeds, fish, and invertebrates.

Cryptocaryon: A ciliated protozoan parasite of marine fish, often observed in aquarium fish that have been recently subjected to stress.

Ecosystem: A large, defined geographic region together with all of its biological components, usually described in relation to the environmental conditions that prevail in the region and which determine the character of the living organisms present.

Element: Substances that cannot be reduced to simpler components by ordinary chemical means.

Flatworm: Any member of the Phylum Platyhelminthes, characterized by a flattened body, simple internal anatomy, and no appendages. They are an important component of a healthy aquarium's microfauna.

Gene flow: The exchange of genetic information that occurs when two non-sibling individuals mate.

The Common Clownfish is by far the most popular species.

Habitat: The geographic location, usually characterized by a specific set of environmental conditions, in which a species is found.

Head and lateral line erosion (HLLE): A condition seen in some species of marine fish, thought to arise as a result of dietary deficiency. Loss of pigment and epidermal tissue on the face and head and along the lateral line, is a characteristic symptom.

Hybridization: Cross-breeding between individuals of different species, or rarely, genera.

Ichthyologist: A biologist specializing in fishes.

Ion: An atom or molecule that has gained or lost one or more electrons, thereby acquiring an electrical charge.

Lateral line: A series of pores, nerve tissue, and canals along both sides of a fish's body that functions in detecting vibrations and water movement, aiding the fish in navigation.

Nutrient: Any organic or inorganic molecule that can be utilized by a living organism for energy production, or as a source of molecular building blocks for growth.

Osmoregulatory: Having to do with maintenance of fluid balance in an organism.

Osmosis: The movement of water molecules across a semi-permeable membrane, such as the membrane surrounding a living cell.

pH: The degree of acidity of a solution, expressed as: $-\log [H^+]$, the negative logarithm of the hydrogen ion concentration in moles per liter. A pH of 7.0 is neutral, lower values are more acidic, higher values more alkaline.

Photoperiod: The number of hours of sunlight to which an organism is exposed daily.

Protogynous hermaphroditism: A form of sex determination in some fish families, in which all juvenile individuals are female. As individuals mature, they may change into males, depending upon environmental circumstances. The opposite phenomenon, in which individuals start life as males and mature into females, is also known and is called "protandrous hermaphroditism."

Salinity: A measurement of the amount of dissolved solids in a solution, expressed in parts per thousand by weight.

Species: Among animals, groups of actually or potentially interbreeding individuals that are reproductively isolated from other such groups.

Substrate: The material on the bottom of an aquarium, or any solid object to which an organism is attached or clings to.

Symbiotic: Referring to any of a variety of relationships in which the ecological roles of two species are related in a complex, specific way.

Taxonomist: A biologist specializing in the naming and description of species, and the elucidation of evolutionary relationships among species.

Venturi: A specially designed tube that mixes air and water via the suction created when water is forced through the tube and encounters a sudden drop in pressure.

Zooxanthellae: Dinoflagellate algae living in an obligate, mutually beneficial symbiotic relationship with certain species of marine invertebrates.

Index

(**Bold** = photo)

71

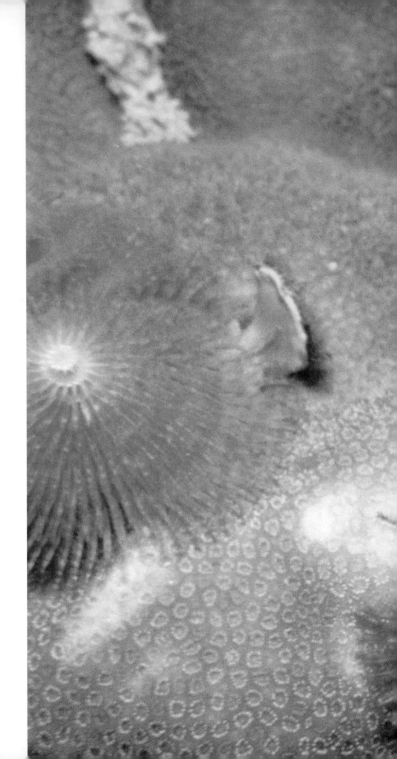

S carcely any other
species of marine
fish can compare with
the Common Clownfish.
Its fascinating relationship
with sea anemones,
pictured here, is detailed
within with beautiful full-
color photographs.